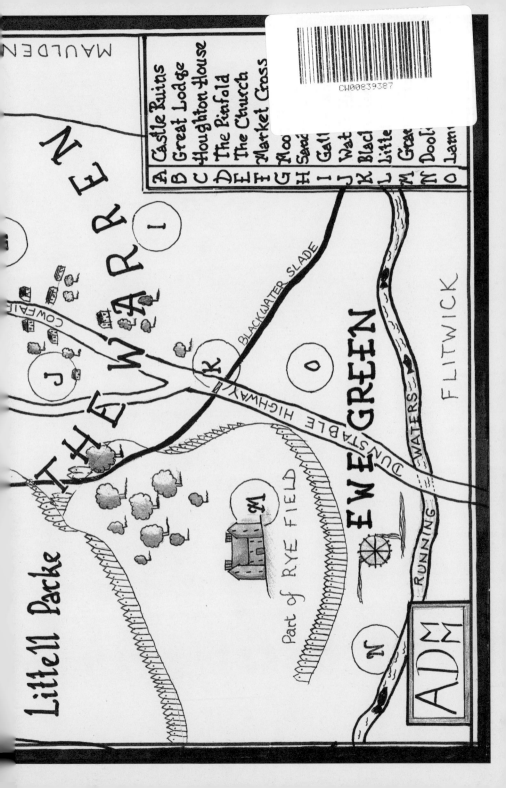

MAULDEN

Littell Parke

THE WARREN

COWFAIR

BLACKWATER SLADE

EWE GREEN

DUNSTABLE HIGHWAY

RUNNING WATERS

FLITWICK

Part of RYE FIELD

ADM

A Castle Ruins
B Great Lodge
C Houghton House
D The Pinfold
E The Church
F Market Cross
G Moo
H Send
I Gatt
J Wat
K Blac
L Litte
M Grea
N Dool
O Lamb

Remember
HUGH REEVE, *Priest,*
fiercely true to his faith
in the face of local persecution,
bigotry and parliamentary censure.
He was Rector of Ampthill from 1600
until his death in 1646.

1600
Hugh Reeve was Presented to the Living of Ampthill by Queen Elizabeth I on 3rd October, Instituted by the Bishop of Lincoln on 13th November and subsequently Inducted by the Archdeacon of Bedford.*

2000
This book was published on 13th November.

*See foot of next page for key.

17th Century Ampthill and
Hugh Reeve, its 'true & lawfull Parson'
by Andrew Underwood

ISBN 0 9508273 5 5

This edition first published in 2000 © Andrew Underwood, Foulislea Cottage, 39 Church Street, Ampthill, Beds. MK45 2PL

Printed by Merry Printers 01582 726959

Key to terminology on previous page
Presentation is the formal nomination of an Incumbent by the Patron of the parish, the Institution is the commission to its spiritual care, and Induction the legal transfer of responsibility for buildings, and the rights to the income and privileges.

17th Century
AMPTHILL
&

Hugh Reeve

its
'true & lawfull Parson'

ANDREW UNDERWOOD

Contents

Illustrations

WITHIN THE TEXT

Thomas 1ˢᵗ Earl of Elgin. Bust formerly on his memorial in the mausoleum at Maulden, drawn by Brenda Bowker, 1956. Page 20
Houghton House from the south H.H.Goodhall, 18ᵗʰ century. Page 28
The Town Houses in Church Square by Ronald L.Holt. Page 47
Sunday no Sabbath, and *Priest's Duty & Dignity* sermons. Pamphlet covers Page 53
Hugh Reeve's register, 1611-1612. Page 60
Henry Page's will. Page 71
Colonel John Okey, the Regicide. Page 85
Ampthill Church from the north, 1817 Page 89

COLOURED PLATES IN CENTRE

1.*Houghton House,* north and west fronts. A lithograph reconstruction (c 1827) by J.Hewetson published in a coloured version by James Smith, Ampthill, 1890.
Staircase from the house, removed to the Swan Inn, Bedford, in 1794.

2. and 3. *House in Church Street once Edmund Wingate's.* Watercolour by Miss F.Emily Barton c1890. Interior 1994. Memorial to Revd Timothy Archer, rector of Meppershall, in the church there. He and his family owned the house from the 1670s to 1742.

4. *Medieval font in Ampthill Church* used in Hugh Reeve's day but removed 1890. Watercolour c1820, perhaps by Thomas Fisher.

5. *Memorial in Ampthill Church* to Richard Nicolls, who named New York, showing the canon ball that killed him in 1672.

6. *1646 wall painting* in the White Hart honouring Charles Prince of Wales.
Pargetting roundel 'WH 1677' in the King's Arms Yard, 1950s, (see page 37).

7. *Ewe Green, Ampthill* in about 1820, by Thomas Fisher. Looking towards Flitwick, the Warren on the left and the Grange on the right, a scene largely unchanged from the 17th century.
Viewed from as close a point as possible, July 2000.

8. *Maulden Church*, with the Bruce Mausoleum as originally constructed under the direction of Benjamin Rhodes.
Conquest Bury (site of Bury Farm in Houghton Conquest) home of Richard Conquest. Early 19th century paintings by Thomas Fisher.

The Thomas Fisher watercolours and the documents on pages 60 and 71 are reproduced by courtesy of the Bedfordshire and Luton Archives and Records Service. All other illustrations are from author's collection.

END PAPER PLAN

Drawn by Anthony Mager (see page 8)

TITLE PAGE AND COVER DESIGNS

from *A Booke of Svndry Dravghtes* . . . *for Glasiers* printed by Walter Dight, 1615.
Hugh Reeve's signature from an original document.
'True & Lawfull Parson' is a quotation from his will – Appendix B.

Preface

This history was written to mark the 400th anniversary of the arrival in Ampthill of a new rector, Hugh Reeve, blissfully unaware of the troubles the next forty-six years would bring him from a vociferous, articulate and influential opposition within his parish and beyond. These were days of unprecedented turmoil in religion and politics (which at that time was the same thing) and in order to appreciate the background to Ampthill life in this period, the *Excursus* on page 97 should be read before anything else. Hugh Reeve was in the tradition of the church which by the 20th century would evolve into a form followed at Ampthill and known as Prayer Book Catholic. Had he lived another couple of years he would have been among 30 like-minded Bedfordshire clergy (2,425 nationally) ejected from their livings during the Commonwealth, when the church was Presbyterian, but reinstated at the Restoration.

The following study has grown out of a lifetime's research into the history of Ampthill conducted chiefly in the 1960s and 1970s in the Bedfordshire County Record Office (now the Bedfordshire and Luton Archives and Records Service) and I am most grateful to the four successive county archivists and their staff for the courtesy, patience and kindness that has always accompanied their help over the years.

Ampthill was Bruce territory through most of the 17th century and until 1738, when the estate was sold to the Duke of Bedford, who acquired the property and manorial records, personal and household records being retained by the Bruces in Wiltshire. In 1971 their Ampthill archive was borrowed for microfilming in Bedford, which gave me an unprecedented opportunity to examine it thoroughly. The Russell papers had been deposited in the record office in 1966, and combined with the Bruce material to form a unique and valuable historical source. Bedfordshire historians will always be indebted to these two families for the stewardship of their archives over so many generations, and for making them available for study.

8

My special thanks are due to Miss Patricia Bell, an assistant in the record office when I made my first visits and ultimately County Archivist, who read the draft of this book with her invariable kindness and good humour, giving sound advice and preventing many a *faux pas*. I am grateful too, to Richard Wildman, the Bedford historian, for his careful scrutiny of the text and for moral and practical support in the project. David Forster undertook the book's technical presentation in the new skills of which he is master, and I thank him for that. Barry Dackombe's technical aid along the way has been vital and much appreciated.

Basic sources for this study are a survey of Ampthill's crown lands made in 1649 and the two earliest maps of the town, which bridge the 17th century (see page 120). Anthony Mager's end paper, which will be of great assistance to readers, is based on these maps and catches the style of the period in a skilful blend of fact and (with some of the buildings) well-informed conjecture.

Particular acknowledgement is due to Peter Chapman, my photographic collaborator for over half a century. He has recorded the town's vicissitudes through that time in a unique and fascinating chronicle, and I am especially grateful to him for providing the colour photographs for this volume.

This being a personal ramble and not a scholarly treatise I have allowed myself to roam outside the strict limits of the title. But I hope I have been able to do justice to Hugh Reeve's memory. It is ironic that the evidence produced to malign him by one faction of what in later years would evolve into a sectarian division, should show him to have been a conscientious parish priest in the tradition they despised. Religion can be a funny business!

Andrew Underwood,
Foulislea Cottage,
Ampthill.
16th August 2000

1

The Tudor Legacy

*'I and my people are well ever since we came to Anthill on Saturday last in
marvellous good health and cleanness of air . . .'*
Henry VIII to Cardinal Wolsey, 14th July 1528

Sometime between 1535 and 1543 Ampthill was visited by a remarkable
travelling antiquarian, John Leland, who had been commissioned to inspect
all the monastic and collegiate libraries and bring what was worthwhile
'out of deadly darkness to lively light' by adding it to the royal library.
The topographical and antiquarian notes he made whilst visiting every
corner of the realm (his *Itinerary*) combined to provide Henry VIII
with a complete account of 'Englandes Antiquities' which he presented
to the king as a New Year's gift in 1546. Leland came to Ampthill via
Willington, 'about xij. miles, almost all by chaumpayn grounde [open
country, no enclosed fields] part by corne, and parte by pasture, and sum
baren hethy and sandy ground. About the castelle [its]self and the toune
of Antehille is faire wood.' He gives a description and history of the
castle, 'now stonding stately on an hille, with four or five faire towers of
stone in the inner warde, beside the basse-courte,' built by Lord Fanhope
(Sir John Cornwall) 'of such spoiles as it is saide that he wonne in
Fraunce'. He concludes 'The market town of Antehill is praty and
welle favoridly buildyd . . . parte of it standeth on a hille, but the most
and the best parte in a valley. There runnith a broket, as I remember, by
the east part of the towne.'[1]

When the new rector Hugh Reeve arrived in the town in 1600 there
might still have been a few of his parishioners who had been alive in the
exciting days of King Henry VIII's involvement in Ampthill life. Some
would have heard from their parents and grandparents of the dramatic

confrontation in the castle drawing room between Queen Katherine and the delegation sent from Archbishop Cranmer's court at Dunstable, formally announcing the annulment of her marriage to the king. When confronted with the document 'she called for penne and ynke, and in such places as she fownde the name Prynces Dowagier,' the new title by which she was to be known, 'she . . . strake yt out, as it ys apparaunt' (to this very day) 'sayeing that she was . . . the Queene, and the Kynges true wife.' They would have remembered the sad day, 17th August, 1533, when the queen was taken from Ampthill, through crowds of distressed well-wishers, to the Bishop of Lincoln's palace at Buckden in Huntingdonshire. It is likely the new rector had been able to supplement their stories with tales of the queen's brief stay at Buckden, since he had been on the bishop's staff there immediately before coming to Ampthill. Poor Katherine* died at Kimbolton castle on 7th January, 1536.

The surrounding countryside would remain substantially unchanged from the time of John Leland's visit until after enclosure at the beginning of the 19th century, but following the death of Henry VIII the castle quickly fell into ruin (helped by townsfolk who raided it for building materials). The crown properties in the town were similarly decrepit and the whole place must have appeared shabby and neglected until James I's hunting interests led to a revival of royal interest and involvement in the area. Significant improvement came with the arrival of the Bruces and the building of stately mansions in Great Park and Houghton Park.

* Katherine *always* wrote her name with an initial 'K'.

2

Around the Town

'I find by Mr Cardonnel's letter to me . . . that he knowes when he is well,
and is not willing to leave so sweet a place as Amthill . . .'
Letter from Lord Devonshire to his cousin Robert, Lord Bruce,
10th November 1652
[Philip de Cardonnel, died 1667, was a fashionable poet]

For Paul Hentzer, a German tourist passing through the county in 1598, Ampthill was the only place worthy of comment, his entire diary entry being: 'a town' where 'we saw immense numbers of rabbits, which are reckoned as good as hares, and are very well tasted.'   He was quite right, as will be seen, for the major part of Ampthill was one vast rabbit warren, tightly regulated and vital to the town's economy until the 19th century.   The soil was too sandy for any crop except rye and hemp, but rabbits and sheep thrived.   Almost three-quarters of the town was surrounded by a vast warren carefully managed on behalf of the lords of the manor, with rabbits being in great demand in the London poultry market at Newgate (where they were sometimes sold '13 to the dozen') and also closer to home.   The 1649 survey estimated it to be about 250 acres 'bounded on the North with greate Parke, and on the West with Little Parke and . . . the highway that leades . . . to Maulden on the Easte, and with Ampthill Towne feildes on the south'.   At that time it was leased by Robert Hewett of the Grange.   In addition, there were private warrens in Great Park and Houghton Park, managed for the occupants of the respective houses, who found them a valuable source of income.

Sometimes the rabbits got out of control, as in 1611, when Parson Reeve, his churchwardens Thomas Kirby and William Savadge and others 'the freholders together with the kinges tennantes, in Consideracion of the distroyeinge of a Bourrowe of Connies [rabbits] heretofore bred to the anoyance of the parishionners' on land between the park and Tilekiln Close (north east of the church), handed the plot over to the king's tenant of the adjoining Long Close, for him to manage. Sometimes temptation got the better of the Ampthill people, as in the next century when Richard Gray would receive a gaol sentence of three months for snaring rabbits in his own garden.[2]

The warreners were given great authority to act against poachers and there were often violent incidents, though fortunately rarely as serious as on 10th January, 1669. 'About three houres before the day' Richard Arnold, keeper, and his assistant Thomas Carter were in the warren when they confronted William Evans and Ambrose Whitamore, obviously poaching. The latter hit Arnold 'three blowes' with his stick 'whereupon hee . . . stood in his defence'. Evans joined in, and Arnold battled on giving Whitamore a 'mortal wound'. They took him off to the Bell in Dunstable Street, together with 'the hay and eleven coneys' that had been poached and Whitamore's stick, which they took to the constable. Richard Arnold and Thomas Carter were charged with murder at the Assizes in 1670.[3]

The Dunstable Highway
Visitors from the south would enter the town by fording the fast-flowing stream, long known as Running Waters, which is now piped under the roundabout on the bypass near Redborne School. This part of Ampthill was known as Ewe (sometimes corrupted to How) Green. On the left they would have noticed Dolittle Mill, in Tudor times also known as Tyldesmylle – presumably because of its superior roofing material. At this time the mill was leased by the crown to Sir Francis Bryan, who held most of the offices giving him responsibility for the management of the Ampthill estates, and would have been worked by one of his tenants. The main highway passed through the Grange, originally a sheep farm belonging to the monks of Warden Abbey but by now farmed by Robert Hewitt, whose family had remained loyal Roman Catholics. On the right, as the visitors climbed the slight rise, was Grange Field (where

Redborne School stands) adjoining Lammas Ground. Adjoining was Charles's Close, and on the opposite side of the road, where Grange Road is now, was Arbour Close. The Grange house stood roughly on the site of Farm Close. Here also was Rye Field (where John Okey had a windmill built in the early 1650s) leading to Little Park and The Moors (later part Ling Hills, now the Firs).[4]

In 1588 there was a serious dispute as to whether Rye Field and Grange Field were part of the warren or not. William Sweyne, the warrener, claimed that they were, while William Huett who farmed the Grange, disagreed. A number of elderly local witnesses were called who all supported the Grange case, among them Edward Middleton, aged 50 'or thereabouts' who had heard his father say that the fields 'dyd belonge to the said Grange tyme out of mynde.' Robert Dennys of Flitwick, husbandman, aged about 72 (supported by Thomas Whyte of Maulden) said that the 'bownde between the said Warren and the saide Grange feilde' was the stream known as Blackwater. A map (now battered, not easy to decipher and with chunks missing) was drawn and filed with the evidence. It marks Blackwater Slade (marshy valley), which now flows unnoticed beneath Flitwick Road, between Grange Road and Holland Road, but in the 1450s when known as Foweysbroke (or Fennesbrook), was dammed to make fish pools. There was a gate across the highway here, and once through it, travellers making for the castle or Great Park or on the way to Woburn, would veer left across the warren over Watch House Hill, where the warreners had their lookout for poachers.

Passing along the bottom of Cow Fair Hill (Briar Close/Lime Road area) they would emerge in the open space known as the Waste (common land belonging to the manor used for pasture – the Sands, as the open space in front of the Alameda gates is called, was probably the last vestige of this) and so into the Woburn Road not far from the site of the present police station.[5]

The main road continued from Blackwater along the line of the present Flitwick Road towards the town centre, the road crossing part of the

Moors and over Galley Nolle ('The Knoll') to a bit more of Rye Field where there was a gate on the Maulden parish boundary. Nearer the town centre were Sanders's Pieces, ancient enclosures now built over and commemorated in Saunders Piece, which are thought to have belonged to Robert Sanders, yeoman (a farmer who owned his land rather than one who rented, however rich) who died in 1608. Passing through Cow Fair End, a traveller would reach the cross roads perhaps noting somewhere on their way the sign of an inn formerly called the Faulcon but in the 1640s the Ragged Staff (the crest of the Greys of Wrest, former owners of the manor of Ampthill). And next door but one to the Red (now White) Hart, another inn, the Bell or Snowe's Place – later the Compasses.

Adjoining the Red Hart on the east side and belonging to the crown, was Old Howse Yard, a dwelling (with garden) obviously of some prestige value to the manor, and probably where the bailiff of the Honour had lived. Next door was a property leased at the time of the 1649 survey to Edmund Wingate for the rent of a red rose – a peppercorn rent with a difference. (Later, the rent of Bury Piece in Dame Ellensbury manor would be £14 a year plus one turkey and six hens. Part of Barnacles, a field off Church Street, was let for a peppercorn in the 1670s.)[6]

The Road to Bedford
The Ampthill soil was particularly suited to the growing of hemp, its fibres being used in the making of coarse cloth and rope. There were hemplands in Dunstable Street at a property (site not yet identified) known as Copt Hall,[7] occupied in 1649 by Richard Gray. But most of its growth seems to have been in Bedford Street, where in the 16th century there was a field called Teynter Close (a tenter is a device for stretching out cloth to set or dry). In the 1640s Thomas Hill leased a cottage, with hempland, on the west side of Bedford Lane, as did his neighbour William Hudson, gentleman, whose extensive brick making interests are mentioned elsewhere. Most important for the trade was the horse mill in what is now Claridge's Lane but was for many years the Rope Walk, where the rope makers worked. In 1577 when its crown lease came up

for renewal the auditor's clerk noted on the survey: 'The premises as I am crediblelie informed are in greate decaye,' but it survived and remained a great asset to the town, so that for several centuries Woburn Street was known as Mill Street.

In Bedford Street was White's Yard, which probably took its name from Henry White who died in 1625 and whose will is detailed below. Here were two tenements and three small pieces of land called Gardin Plottes which belonged to the crown as part of the manor and were what would soon become known as market gardens. There were other Gardin Plottes in Bedford Street and elsewhere in the town. Those journeying to Bedford might catch a glimpse of the Great Lodge (on the site of Park House) from the top of the hill as they passed into Hazelwood Lane. This was quite a formidable stretch of road, always in need of repair, but there was a convenient spring of fresh water at the bottom of the hill where travellers could refresh themselves. From 1615 they would not have failed to look to their right and marvel at the magnificence of Lady Pembroke's new mansion. Once the Abbot of Reading's wood was reached, the road passed into the parish of Houghton Conquest. [8]

The Town Centre
At the crossroads in the middle of the town was the ancient Moot Hall, a half-timbered two storey building accessible from all sides, probably built in the 1440s, with an upper room and little shops on the ground floor. Old documents refer to a Market Cross standing near the Moot Hall, but no details of its age or design exist, neither is its precise site known. However, the 1743 warren map shows a rectangular building, surely intended to be the Moot Hall, in front of which is a taller 'pepper-pot' structure with a small lantern or finial on its sloping roof which could well have supported a cross at one time. It appears to have two storeys, with door at ground level and two windows above, similar to some village lock-ups. This is surely the Market Cross, probably used for storing market gear and serving as town lock-up until a new one was built in Bedford Street as part of Lord Ossory's Market Square reorganisation in the 18th century.

There is nothing from Ampthill town centre of the 1600s that a present day townsman would recognise. The four main streets follow the same line, and many buildings occupy ancient sites and have at their core parts that were already very old. But 18th century refronting, when timber framing was hidden behind neat brickwork, leaded lights gave way to orderly sash windows (real or pretend) and the ground floor was brought into line with the overhanging upper storey, changed the scene totally.[9]

The Road from Millbrook
The boundary between Ampthill and Millbrook is on the western side of Westminster Pond, and the highway here was known as Ware (short for Warren) Lane. The Tudor map is quite clear that this is the 'Highway from Owburne to Ampthill Towne' and shows it passing through the carefully drawn palings of the royal Great and Little Parks, on either side of the road. A short distance from the road within Little Park was a spring known as Tander's - a corruption of Saint Andrew's - Well. A sacred spring in pagan times (its waters were said to be particularly beneficial to eye complaints) it had been converted to Christian use in the name of the town's patron saint. Nearer the town the road became Slutts End alias the Waste, and from the top of the hill into the town was for centuries called Mill Street.

Church Street
The Ampthill of King Henry's day is likely to have been well maintained and orderly, but his immediate successors took no special interest in the town. Surviving rentals for the 1570s and 1580s report serious decay, a typical example being two cottages in Church Street, annual rent 20 shillings for both, which the clerk reported to be 'in greate decaye for wante of Reparacions for lacke of timber . . . so as tenne poundes [i.e. ten years' rent] will not suffice for the repayre thereof and there ys noe tymber to bee had growinge upon the premisses'. And it was the same story – and worse – at many other properties elsewhere in the town.[10]

One Church Street property in pristine condition at this time would be the gentleman's house at what is now numbered 31 to 35A. Richard

Hodgkis, gentleman, steward of the Honour of Ampthill from 1616 was living there with his wife Elizabeth (who died in 1624) when he took over the lease and management of the market stalls. About ten years later Arthur Hodgkis, pewterer and citizen of London (and presumably their son) sold the house and four acres of grounds to Edmund Wingate, mathematician and legal writer (Chapter 7) who had been appointed warden, bailiff and coroner for the Honour of Ampthill by Queen Henrietta Maria. Although Edmund Wingate died in 1656 his family continued to own the property until about 1664 when it passed to Edward Backwell.

By 1670 the house belonged to the Revd Timothy Archer, rector of Meppershall, who like Hugh Reeve, was the target of puritan criticism. Mr Archer was ejected from his living during the Commonwealth and for a time imprisoned in the Fleet prison in London but later restored to his parish where he died in 1672. The following year his widow, Rebecca, gave a 4½ year lease of the Church Street house to Simon Urlin, gentleman, Lord Ailesbury's attorney, but later lived there herself. At her death in 1685, the house passed to her daughter Frances, wife of John Watson of Little Park. Ultimately, their eldest son George, born at Little Park in 1653, inherited the house where he lived for most of his long life – he died in 1742.

George Wateson (he always included the *e* and probably pronounced his name Wattison) became rector of Millbrook but was ejected from the living as a Nonjuror – one of about 400 clergy who refused to take the oath of allegiance to William and Mary in 1688 on the grounds that this would break the oath previously sworn to James II, then living in exile.[11]

Brick Kilns Galore
By the 17th century the fields north of Church Street and into Dame Ellensbury Park were pock-marked with clay pits and tile or brick kilns and there is strong evidence of brick and tile making in the town from the 1400s. A survey in 1542 had noted a Tylekylne being worked by William Eperall on lands to the north and east of the church, while another

kiln closer to the road and east of Church Square had been left to Henry Crouch by Thomas Bredyman in 1557. Henry Crouch bought the adjoining house in Church Square from Peter Grey Esq., and passed it on to his son William in 1590. It changed hands again in 1608 and 1614 and was mortgaged for £25 in 1648 by Edmund Ruffhead, gentleman (Hugh Reeve's son-in-law) to Richard Evans, a brickmaker. In the 1690s George Webb had a brick kiln in Little Park and was able to supply the builders of the John Cross's Ampthill Hospital.

A large field north and east of the church known as Barnacles (10 acres in 1658) and an adjoining close on the west called Barnwick contained another tile kiln 'with an orchard, garden, close of pasture land, meadow and appurtenances' which passed into the hands of Lee Sadler the Younger in the 1650s, and ultimately became a part of Lord Ailesbury's estate. The close or meadow was known as Pond or Moat Close, and borders the main road with the Duck Riddy stream running through it. Lee Sadler built a house here which is clearly marked on the Warren map of 1743. In 1676 it was identified as that 'wherein the Lady Conquest, Elizabeth Dennis, widow (now the wife of Thomas Biggs, Gent.) and the Widow Jeffrey now or lately dwelt.' It is thought the house was demolished in the 19th century, when the whole of Moat Close was excavated for its clay.

With the building of Houghton House and the development of its estate (including the walled kitchen garden and the Lodge House and its garden wall) there was an enormous demand for bricks. In addition, fashion and expediency demanded the refronting of almost all the old houses in the town and the building of many new ones. There were brick kilns in the two royal parks, and a major enterprise in Houghton Park at what is still known as Brick Hill Pastures. In the 1680s the steward noted that William Hudson, gentleman, was tenant of one of a house 'with brickhill & brickhill yard' and that he received wood from the estate for firing the kilns in return for bricks and tiles. 'I have beside the liberty of making 100,000 . . . bricks and tiles at 12d a 1000' adds the steward, pleased at having negotiated a special discount.[12]

The main drive to Houghton House, often known as South Gate Walk, left the Maulden Road at what is now Gas House Lane. Here Duck Riddy stream flowed beneath its ramshackle bridge. On the north side of the road running up to the Maulden boundary was Pinfold Hill alias Little Warren. The Pinfold (where straying cattle were im*pounded* – hence the pound) being at the roadside there. Green Hedges stands on the site and retains in its garden what is thought to have been the pound's sandstone well house. Until the early 1600s when Houghton House was built, the crown owned a farm in this area called John of Ampthill's. The adjoining park was in a separate manor overlapping Ampthill, Maulden and Houghton Conquest, which originated in Norman times with the St Armand family and was called Dame Ellensbury, after Dame Eleanor St Armand.

The London Road

People going to London would travel through Maulden – more often than not on foot or if they could afford the hire, mounted on donkey or horse, or in the comfort of a cart. The usual route would cut across the moor to Hollington Bridge (Thomas Gardiner had left some money towards its upkeep in 1544) where until the 1960s was a waterfall known as Hollington Basin. From there the road led through Newbury to Silsoe and Wrest, and so over the top of the downs at Barton and onwards through the market town of Luton.

Later in the century the household accounts for Houghton House record frequent journeys to London and back. Footmen (literally) living in and with all found, usually received an annual salary of £4 and a tip at the conclusion of a successful journey. William Ansell was sent up with a hackney horse and came back on foot, for which he received 4s. 0d. equivalent to a twentieth part of his annual salary. Going to a funeral in Wimbledon involved opening two tollgates (a shilling) and 'boats for my Lord and Lady' when they crossed the Thames. 'The litter my Lady came to Town in' cost £4 to hire and 5 shillings 'to the Litter man to drink'. (In 1688 Mr Walker was paid £29 for a new velvet Sedan Chair.) In 1683 Crouch and Tom Honour (a faithful retainer) had 9s.0d for taking horses and a cow to London – and presumably walking back. Later, when Tom was seriously ill, he was boarded out in town '6 weeks 3 days at nurse 7s a week'. Dr Symcotts came twice (he was often used for the family and household) and received a pound.

In the summer the household made frequent use of the Silsoe coach. It was a slow trek and sometimes hazardous. This was quite a busy route,

Thomas Bruce, 1ˢᵗ Earl of Elgin, from his memorial Bust (attributed to John Bushnell) formerly in the family mausoleum at Maulden. Drawn in 1956 by Brenda Bowker. Lord Ailesbury above was his namesake and grandson.

as Lord Ailesbury discovered in the early 1690s, when released on bail from the Tower of London where he had been confined on treason charges as a suspected Jacobite sympathiser (which he was). He thought a quiet and unheralded return to Houghton House on borrowed horses would be diplomatic, but at St Albans he was overtaken by Bedfordshire graziers returning from the Friday market at Smithfield, who spread the news. Consequently the church bells in all the villages he passed through were rung, and he was 'met by great numbers on horseback on Luton downs . . . and at a bridge above one mile from my house [probably Hollington Bridge] there were upwards of 3000 on horses and on foot cutting down branches from the trees although without leaves, and strewing rushes and flags with all exclamations of joy . . . a company of Scotch foot [soldiers shouting] huzzas in their highland language.'

3

The Three Parks

*In 1646 Lady Devonshire 'being much depressed in mind with such a load
of publick calamaties, she would try if privacy might give ease to any part
of her sorrows. Retire therefore she did to... Ampthill, a place, if any in the
world ... that could compose her distracted thoughts.'*
Thomas Pomfret in his 'Life of the.Countess Dowager of Devonshire' 1685

Great Park was enclosed by Sir John Cornwall who early in the 15th
century purchased the manor of Ampthill from the St Amand family.
He was a hero of the French wars, particularly Agincourt (1415) where
he had been a commander in the English army and was later in charge
of the occupying force. His wife was Henry IV's sister, the Princess
Elizabeth of Lancaster, and using the considerable wealth he had acquired
during his French campaigns, he built a castle in their new park at Ampthill
appropriately impressive to reflect his personal distinction and royal
connections. The Princess died in 1426, Cornwall (by then Lord Fanhope)
in 1443, their only son having predeceased them the park and castle
passed to Lord Edmund Grey of Wrest, in 1454. Lord Grey (later 1st
Earl of Kent) managed the property well, but his grandson Richard was
a gambler and wastrel, and in 1508 was obliged to forfeit the Ampthill
estate to Henry VII in default of a debt. In due time Henry VIII
succeeded his father, and by making Ampthill a favourite base, brought
the town into prominence.

Henry's passion for hunting was the main attraction, and Ampthill was
run with this a prime concern. The deer were bred in Little Park and
shunted across the road to Great Park when they were mature enough
for hunting, which was done mainly on foot and with the use of dogs.
Ladies and the less agile (or willing) were placed in a pavilion known as

The Stand and equipped with bows and arrows to take pot shots at the deer as they were driven past by the hunters on foot. (In July 1532 Cardinal du Bellay, at Ampthill on state business, reported his friendship with the king and that sometimes the king placed him and 'Madame Anne' [Boleyne] together in the Stand with their cross-bows to shoot the deer as they pass, and in other places to see the coursing . . . Lady Anne had presented him with 'a hunting frock and hat, horn and greyhound . . .') The young Edward VI had been to Ampthill for the hunting, and on at least one occasion his sister Elizabeth came too, but when she became Queen Ampthill was avoided and it was left to her successor James I to revive the practice. The 1649 survey noted a 'new brick building called the stand scituate on the chief hill in the Parke neere unto Ampthill warren on the south for the view of the game being a square of 15 foote and 20 foote in hight [with a] lower and an upper room .' The 1743 warren map positions the Stand not far from the top of Breakheart Hill.[13]

In 1649 the parliamentary commissioners estimated that Great Park comprised 392 acres in Ampthill, 188 acres in Millbrook and 70 acres in 'Hoton' – 650 acres in all – 200 of which were 'mowing or pasture ground', 250 just 'pasture' and 200 warren. (In 1947 Ampthill Urban District Council purchased 156 acres of Great Park for the use of the town, for just under £11,000.)

Ampthill Towers
The castle Sir John Cornwall had built and where Queen Katherine languished is not very well documented and no contemporary illustrations have come to light. Some very sketchy 16th century plans are difficult to relate to written descriptions. J.D.Parry writing in 1827 describes plans which Lord Ossory thought were made in about 1616 'at which time it was supposed the Castle was demolished'. He describes a large outer court presumably covering an area from close to the present Woburn Road to a gateway with two towers leading into smaller courts at the top of the hill. 'In front were two square projecting towers; and round the building, at irregular distances were nine others, projecting, of different

shapes, but principally five-sided segments of octagons – if this description be intelligible.' [14]

In about 1820 Thomas Fisher attempted a sketch reconstruction based on Leland's description and his own interpretation of what was left of the ruins, but a report of the 1580s probably gives the best idea of the castle's layout and condition as time and the plundering of building materials by Ampthill entrepreneurs began to speed its decay. 'The manor house of Ampthill in most part of the inner court is sore decayed in tiling and leading and the battlements of stone sore decayed and most of the glass windows clean gone, and the stone walls much shaken and chiefly the great kitchen and diverse spouts of lead broken and some clean gone. Item in the outer court there, all the timber of all the roofs of the houses must be new, for some of them are clean fallen down, and the tile broken, and the roof ready to fall. Item the old barn in the outer court is ready to fall down because the timber work is rotten and part of the tile broken and gone.' [15]

Musters
Nevertheless the castle would have been used in the last years of Queen Elizabeth's reign by the Lord Lieutenant, Henry Earl of Kent, for mustering the militia 'all armed by the said Erle . . . to be imployed in her Majesties service in Ireland'. In 1598 he impressed 184 soldiers comprising 41 pikemen (including William North of Ampthill), 23 halberdiers, 60 'muskatiers' and 60 'Calivers', with Ampthill's Thomas Chawner among the musketeers and Thomas Hollidaie with the cavalry. 'Fiftie hable footemen' mustered the next winter included Thomas Pollard. Thomas Wilkinson was amongst the 15 'hable men' despatched just before Christmas in 1600, while the '20 Soldiours' sent out to Ireland in May 1602 included William Lambert and Peter Davie. Having been handed into the charge of an officer the soldiers were expected to be at the port in Chester within eight days. [16]

Forty years later, in October 1644, the castle would have been the rendezvous for parliamentary troops responding to the letter from the county committee to the constables of the Willey hundred ordering 'all Trayned Souldiers and supplies and all other persons . . . to appear at Ampthill with their Horses and Armes (with ammunition) upon Tuesday next by nine of the Clocke in the forenoone . . .' By 1649 the castle was said to have been 'totally demolished', but its site continued to provide an area for military parades, camps and exercises through to the 20th century, most notably in the camp set up by the Duke of Bedford in World War I.[17]

Great Lodge
When Ampthill Castle was in its hey day the routine management of the estate was in the hands of the steward and keeper of the parks whose official residence, on the site of the present Park House, was known as Great Lodge. Because of the ruinous state of the castle royal visitors from the late 1540s onwards were accommodated in Great Lodge, among them Edward VI whose visit triggered a frenzied six weeks of repair to the shooting butts, seats and bowling alley. But during the long reign of Queen Elizabeth I only routine maintenance seems to have been undertaken, the house being then occupied by the current steward or his deputy intent on preserving the Queen's deer and game from the attention of poachers both local and from further afield.

The 1649 survey describes Great Lodge as a 'substanciale brick building . . . the length 69 foot . . . breadth 49 ½ foot . . . the hight from wall plate to the ground 21foot . . . the roof being very good timber work & substancially tiled carrying 5 stack of faire brick chimneys'. There was a large entrance hall downstairs, 26 feet by 14 feet with a 19ft square parlour at each end, one completely wainscotted the other partially, and a 'faire' entrance porch. At the back (on the north side) were 'four other lodging Chambers one Pantry and necessary Closet below stairs, one faire large Staircase of Joyners worke leading up into a faire dining Chamber situate over the said hall . . . and six other faire Chambers above staires . . . with Convenient Clossetts . . .' nearly all panelled. An adjoining two-storey timber framed building with brick infilling 40 feet by 30 feet contained two kitchens, a washhouse, bakehouse, buttery with other small rooms. A brewhouse stood to the south of the house, and there was a new brick stable with hayloft, a granary and small hay barn. 'The front to the southward is beautified with a Convenient Courtyard and a garden or young orchard on the west . . . and a kitchen garden at the east end thereof which . . .are surrounded with a new sawen pale.'

The position of the castle perched on the escarpment impressed James I greatly, and in 1606 he had John Thorpe draw up plans for a new great house on the same site, but the scheme fell through and the king had to be satisfied with an enlargement of Great Lodge. Early attention was given to the construction of a wine and beer cellar, which may survive beneath the present building, although the lodge itself, which stood against what is now the north front of the house, was demolished during the remodelling of the 1770s.

James was an enthusiastic hunter and when possible would come into Bedfordshire in alternate years to enjoy the sport. He was also the last great falconer of the kings of England, although hawking was impossible within Ampthill Park owing to density of the woods, even after the drastic felling of the 16th century. But it was 'fair game' for those who had a mind to it. When Charles I came to the throne in 1625, his new warrant to the keeper, Lord Bruce, emphasised the king's regrets at finding the fishing, falconry and venery 'much decayed and distroied by divers gentlemen and other inhabitants . . . who with Hawkes, Nettes, Gunnes, Buckstaules, Greyhoundes, Setting d(og)ges Lowbells, Beagles, Stuckle Currs, Crosbowes, Snares and other Engines as well for the night as the daie have very much impaired the same . . .' Lord Bruce is ordered to search them out, ' . . . especially in the night season', confiscate their weapons and take them before the Justices of the Peace for appropriate punishment. By 1649 the red deer of Tudor days had been replaced by 76 fallow deer.

Timber Harvest
In the 16th and 17th centuries the real treasure of the parks was in its oak

trees, a harvest of incalculable value planted with great faith and foresight when Sir John Cornwall created the park early in the 1420s and nurtured over many generations. By the time John Leland noted the 'faire wood' surrounding the castle the trees would have been about a century old, in a closely planted wood with sufficient distance between the trees to allow the deer to roam and be hunted. Although Queen Elizabeth showed little interest in her Ampthill estate, her government was very conscious of it as an asset, and the state papers through several reigns record careful attention to the oaks and their management. There was a great deal of Ampthill in the 'Wooden Walls of England' and other national and local structures. Between 1583 and 1598 2,018 Ampthill oaks were felled for Crown use and when the 1649 survey was prepared the commissioners found 400 trees recently 'marked with the three Anchors' for navy use, with others surviving from an earlier selection 'marked for the use of the Navy by the armes of England'. 2,000 more trees were 'for the most part old Doterells & decayed . . . good for little save the fire', although some grand specimens survived into the 20th century.

Little Park

Little Park was the breeding ground for the deer destined for hunting in Great Park, so the keeper was a person of importance and authority. Most crown offices at this time were leased out, often to royal servants who supplemented their salary – if they had one – by sub-letting to others who actually did the work. In 1553, for example, Queen Mary had made a grant for life 'to Thomas Borage, the queen's cook,' of the 'office of parker of Little Park . . . custody of the lodge within the park . . . [and] master of the chace of wild beasts and deer etc within the park and 20 feet around.'   The early occupants of the lodge included Sir Thomas Hillersden, whose wife Elizabeth was buried at Ampthill in 1616. He was knighted 1622 but died the following year and was buried at Elstow where his family held the manor and built a palatial house (long in ruins) in the priory building.   His will records that he was a friend of Bruces, and in particular Francis Nicolls and his wife Margaret (nee Bruce) whom he appointed his overseers, leaving them 40 shillings to buy a mourning ring. [18]

In the 1680s the Little Park lodge was described as 'a very faire house with a garden walled about, a large dove house with barnes stables & all convenient out houseing. Also several fish ponds'. Back in the 1640s it had been the home of the recusant Richard Watson, and an inventory of his possessions lists the rooms. On the ground floor was the hall, a parlour, middle parlour, and inner parlour, with the kitchen and 'milk house'. Upstairs were rooms over the larder, kitchen, hall, parlour and cellar (sic). Also upstairs were the great chamber, a little chamber, the clocke chamber (interesting, did the house have a turret clock?) closet, and a garret. (It is tempting to think that a small upstairs room, probably the closet of the 1643 inventory, beautifully panelled in oak (now lost), was an oratory where Father Augustine Baker said his prayers and 'one Adkynson, the olde papyste preste' known to have been sheltered by the Watsons ministered to the local recusants.)

Outside was the brewhouse and servant's house with the men's chamber, the bayliff's chamber, a little closet, and the cheeseloft. The 1671 Hearth Tax returns record 15 fireplaces at Little Park, and the same number at Richard Emery's in Ewe Green (the Grange), second to Lord Ailesbury, who had 55 hearths, a difficult assessment to equate with the steward's ledger entry five years later: 'Chimney money 68 about the house, 14 in Great Park, £4.2s.' [19]

The recusant Richard Watson noted above was followed at Little Park by his second son John who conformed to the Church of England, probably when he married Frances daughter of the scholarly Revd Timothy Archer (rector of Meppershall) and his wife Rebecca (later of Church Street, Ampthill). John and Frances Watson remodelled the house, enclosing the original Tudor building in a brick casing and their initials are still to be seen on the rainwater heads

Dame Ellensbury (Houghton) Park
The manorial system did not take account of parish boundaries. Steppingley, for example, came under four manors each holding its own

28

court and with its own lord to acknowledge and its own regulations to
obey. Ampthill was more fortunate in that from 1366 most of the town
fell within one manor. But a large portion of the north eastern corner of
the parish was part of a manor largely centred on Houghton Conquest
and known as Dame Ellensbury. In the early years of the 15th century
it was held jointly by Almaric St Amand and his wife Eleanor, the Dame
Ellen after whom it is named. Thanks to Dame Eleanor's stewardship
her park matched Great Park for its deer and its game, and from Tudor
times it came under the same management. In the early 1600s Dame
Ellensbury Park was held by Sir Edmund Conquest, whose family lived
at Conquest Bury (site of Bury Farm, Houghton Conquest), but in 1615
James I granted the park to Mary Herbert, the countess of Pembroke,
(see Chapter 6) who built a stately house on the north face of the
greensand ridge.[20]

Houghton House
*18th century engraving of the south front by H.H.Goodhall. Note 'I.R.' (Jacobus
Rex) carved over central doorway, sundials beneath gable windows on third
floor, and a turret with weathervane from the east front. No full view of the
east front has as yet come to light. For north and west fronts, see Plate 1.*

The commanding position of Lady Herbert's stately mansion gives it
clear views in all directions and even as a ruin it remains an impressive

and dramatic building. The house was built of red brick (almost certainly made on the estate) with facings of the local stone, Totternhoe Clunch. There were three storeys with the principal rooms on the first floor and facing north. On the north and west fronts were classical loggias (added very early in the house's history) with triple arcades of pillars, the latter carrying heraldry relating to the Sidneys, Dudleys and Herberts, and on the south front a projecting brick porch reaching the whole height of the building. This bore the initials IR – Jacobus Rex, thought to commemorate a visit made by King James in 1621. Square towers at the corners were surmounted by concave roofs supporting pinnacles with gilded finials. Heavily ornamented brick chimneys rose above the roof-line and a basement under the eastern part contained the kitchens and other offices.[21]

Lady Pembroke died in September 1621, two months after King James had visited her. Within a short time her son surrendered the park to the king who granted it to Lord Thomas Bruce, who also purchased the house. The Bruce family were to continue living here until 1738, when it was bought by the Duke of Bedford and dismantled in 1794. It is not clear when the mansion became known as Houghton House (it is in Ampthill parish, just, the boundary with Houghton running along the north wall). John Aubrey, writing in the middle of the 17th century, calls it Houghton Lodge. In the 1760s it was known as Ampthill House, the name adopted at different times by two other properties.

Postscript
In 1646, when Charles I was desperately in need of money to finance his army in the civil war, he borrowed £12,912 from John Ashburnham (1603-1671) and two others, using Ampthill, Brogborough and Beckerings parks as security. Ashburnham, who had been MP for Hastings, and was then treasurer and paymaster of the Royalist army, paid off the debt to his colleagues and on the Restoration of Charles II was granted a barony and a 40 year lease on the estates for his work in supporting the royal cause. In 1675 Charles II, keeping a promise made by his father, granted the parks to Ashburnham's son (also John) absolutely. [22]

4

Town Life

*'We have the best Prince and the best Laws: and both are to be defended
from the evil and ingratefull treatments of malicious Adversaries.'*
From a sermon 'Subjection for Conscience-sake' preached at the Assizes
held at Ampthill in 1682, by Thomas Pomfret, Vicar of Luton,
Chaplain to Robert Earl of Ailesbury.

Ampthill's increasing prosperity through the 17th century owed much to
residents who had settled in the town to administer its royal manor, and
from the 1620s to the presence of the Bruces at Houghton House and
the professional staff they employed to run their estate. The crown's
interest in Ampthill as a source of revenue was significant, and important
to the town's development. In 1542 Henry VIII had combined the
considerable number of manors he had recently acquired in 45 parishes
in Bedfordshire and the adjoining counties (mostly from the monasteries)
into an administrative group under the title the Honour of Ampthill. The
rents and other profits from the honour were set apart to provide an
income for his fourth wife, Anne of Cleves, who died in 1557.

James I settled the honour on Charles Prince of Wales, who made it
over to his new wife the Princess Henrietta Maria and she appointed its
officers and received its income as Queen for the rest of her life –
except during the Commonwealth, when it was bought by Colonel John
Okey (an officer in the parliamentary army) and some of his colleagues.
After Queen Henrietta Maria's death in 1669, the honour was let on a
long lease to Thomas Bruce, Earl of Ailesbury whose family sold it in
1730 to the Duke of Bedford, a descendant buying the outstanding rights
from the Crown in 1881[23]

Manor Court
Town life was to an extent run by the court baron of the lord of the manor, which usually met in the Moot Hall. Unfortunately the records of its proceedings for the 17th century have not survived, but typical examples of offenders and their fines from the previous century are quoted elsewhere. The appointment of the manor's officers and their functions would not have changed by the 18th century when records begin again. The steward presided as deputy for the lord of the manor and the proceedings opened with a proclamation read three times and ending with a roll call of tenants. Changes of property ownership through sales, death or inheritance, were noted on the court roll, a copy being given to the new owner (hence copyhold). Bylaws for the management of the warren, common, open fields and public areas of the town were then made, and officers appointed to uphold them. All officers were unpaid, and expected to do their duty in addition to the daily work which provided their living. The bellman (night watchman and town crier) however, kept the fee he levied for crying public calls.

The constable usually served for a year (Ampthill had two) and was sometimes the subject of personal assault. The afferer's job was to assess the fines levied by the court, and the field driver and the hayward (often the same person) would round up straying cattle, put them in the pound (pinfold), control the open and common fields and make sure fences were in good repair. Sometimes there was a leather sealer, whose job was to check on the work of the tanners. One man usually combined the offices of ale-taster, flesh searcher and butter weigher, the forerunner of the inspector of weights and measures as it became in the 1790s.

Markets and Fairs
In 1219 Henry III had granted the lord of the manor a charter for a weekly market to be held on a Thursday, and this was confirmed later in his reign (1242) with additional authority to hold an annual fair on the eve, feast and morrow of Saint Mary Magdalene, 21st to 23rd July. Other fairs were authorised over the centuries and flourished or dwindled as

the town's needs changed so that by the 1640s there were two – Saint Andrew's Day (the town's patron saint) 30th November, and Saint George's Day, 23rd April. Later in the 17th century, it was decided to revive the July fair and encourage support for the market for 'cattel & comodities' by making it toll free for two years. At this time the market was set up 'betweene the Red hart Inne & the King's Arms Inne' (until this point known as the Crown) and straggled along the streets from the Oxlet, where the butchers had their shambles, to Cowfair End (Dunstable Street) where the cattle market took place. Sheep were traded along Mill Street and into Slutts End. A Market Place was created in 1784 by clearing some old buildings from the town centre, when Lord Ossory erected the town pump and oversaw the erection of a new Market House with a sheltered colonade for dealers on the site of the old one, which had 'tumbled down'.[24]

The income from tolls at markets and fairs was a valuable asset of the lord of the manor and so was leased out to someone in the town who owned the actual stalls and paraphernalia and was responsible for routine administration. When Ambrose Samm, yeoman, died in 1659 his will recited his title to the 14 'Market Stalls . . . & the Butchers Shambles late in the tenure of Edward Blofeild, bailiff' which Samm held 'by right of indenture 7 May 1631 between himself and Arthur Hodgkis, citizen & pewterer of London', and in particular 'all my stallyeares bonds, the stalls, crutches, poles & other implements used in the said Fairs and Markett.' [25]

The markets and fairs brought many outsiders to the town, and that was their main purpose. Speculation is no substitute for history, but it is more than likely that in the 1630s the small boy John Bunyan came touting for business at Ampthill market with his father Thomas, the Elstow brazier. After a spell (perhaps) in the parliamentary army towards the end of the civil war, Bunyan set up in business on his own account, would have visited the town on many occasions, and from the 1650s would have been known here as a preacher. It is possible also that in the 1640s the blacksmith's son from Ickwell, Thomas Tompion, visited the markets and fairs here from time to time. He grew up to be 'the father of English watch and clock-making'. (Robert Bruce MP, of Houghton House, had a gold watch of Mr Tompion in 1712 for £26.) Both Bunyan and Tompion were boys from very ordinary Bedfordshire backgrounds who achieved extraordinary fame in very different disciplines. [26]

Hospitality

The town's three coaching inns were the Swan in Mill Street (later the King's Head, 3 Woburn Street), the Crown (later the Kings Arms, 9 Church Street) and appropriately for Ampthill (with its three parks well stocked with deer) the Hart. By 1649 this had become the Red Hart and went White in about 1677, although known by either colour until about 1739, when it was refronted. Next door but one from the Red Hart along Dunstable Street was the Bell, an ancient hostelry with records going back to the 15th century. Sometimes known as Snowe's Place (Elizabeth Snow was the 'alehouse keeper' in 1500) it became the Compasses early in the 18th century and survived as such until 1911. (Barclay's Bank cash point marks the spot.) In the 1640s the Bell was owned by John Franklin, Ralph Saye being the keeper.

The 1649 survey of crown lands describes the Red Hart as being 40 feet in length and 18 feet deep with two cellars (still there) and on the ground floor a kitchen, hall, parlour, room over one of the cellars, two other small rooms. Upstairs were four chambers (public rooms) and two 'Clossettes'. Elsewhere 'a small Brewehouse, two stables, a Woodhouse, one Barne, one Granery on the backside . . . two small Gardins, one Orchard, one pightell [small field or enclosure] of pasture with the back yard – 2 acres.' Thomas Bussey, gentleman, was the occupant and he held it by letters patent from James I in 1616 to Jeffrey Palmer, who had died in 1619 when an inventory of his property was made. This lists the contents of each room, which includes in the wine cellar sack, claret and muscadine and a plentiful supply of beer. Bedclothes included 20 pairs each of flaxen, holland and canvas sheets for use in the Red Chamber, the Great Chamber and the Gatehouse Chamber. The nine pewter candlesticks and nine pewter chamber pots suggest maximum overnight accommodation. His silver gilt plate included four bowls and 'two dozen of silver spones unguilt'. In the yard was 'a henn penne or coope' and in the stable, amongst other oddments 'five hives of bees . . . three porklings . . . two barrow hoggs . . . three sowes . . . six piggs' and elsewhere 'seaven kyne . . . two nages . . . a mare and a coult . . .' the total value being £520.6s.8d.[27]

Postal Arrangements
The first public postal service was set up in 1635 on a direct route between London and Edinburgh, the mail being dropped off at specific points or stages – hence stage coaches. Five years later this had been increased to eight lines, spreading out from London across the country. Bedfordshire letters were left or received at Brickhill on the Watling Street and collected for distribution by the local carriers. (In 1652 Robert Lord Bruce wrote to his aunt: 'on a carrier's day our rurall tranquility is discomposed both by publique & private Intelligence'. The Houghton House accounts record a 2s 6d Christmas box to the post boy.) In 1677 a branch post was established to Bedford and extended the following year through Ampthill and Luton to London three times a week, the Ampthill post house being the White Hart. The cost of sending a letter depended on the number of pages and how many stages it passed through. [28]

Childhood Perils
John Franklin who owned the Bell and other properties in the town had a son, christened John in 1641, who was asthmatic. Robert Woodcock, the Ampthill physician, was friendly with Dr John Symcotts who lived in Huntingdon where his patients included Oliver Cromwell and his family. Symcotts also had a practice in Bedfordshire, attended family and staff at Houghton House, and was frequently in the area professionally in the civil war. Some of his notebooks have survived, among them that for 1650 where he wrote: 'A son of Mr Jo. Francklin's of Ampthill, being mightily stuffed and in an asthmatical fit and ready to be choked, took salad oil by spoonfuls, and when he could not speak pointed for it, and it eased him in a very short space.' [29]

Less fortunate was ten-year-old John Copeland, son of William the Ampthill butcher, who in 1677 was 'gatheringe of nutts' in Wootton with two of his sisters in the care of Mary Freelove, widow. She told how they had been accosted by Robert Butt of Wootton, labourer, 'with a great dogg & he being in wrath with [them] for gatheringe of nutts . . . maniged the dogg to run upon the said John Copeland so that upon feare thereof [he] did cry out . . . '   Robert Butt said 'good boy bee not afraid'.   But when John got back home 'verie much affrighted' his father 'demanded of him the cause thereof & when he came to himselfe hee told him it was occationed by a dogg as run att him as hee was gathering of nutts . . . And afterwards hee asked of him if the dogg had bitten him & he replied hee had received noe wound by the said dogg.' Edward Bouskill the Ampthill apothecary had been sent for and reported to the court that 'John was then very sick & is now dead. And that hee did conceive the said childe was in a kind of a violent feavoure but noething of appearance of any wound upon any part of his body according as it might bee supposed to bee don by a dogg.'

Food and Drink
John Copeland would have been gathering nuts from that versatile and valuable tree, the hazel. When properly coppiced it was widely used in building, particularly in the making of panels for wattle and daub infilling, and for hurdles and fencing. It converted well into charcoal – and its twigs were used in dowsing (which the puritans would condemn as witchcraft). Above all it produced a nutritious and tasty nut which, formed an important part of the everyday diet. (The gravediggers who prepared a vault at the entrance to the chancel very early in the 18th century left evidence of their lunch in the form of sheep and ox bones, chestnut skins and clay pipe fragments.) [30]

The diet for most people would by present day standards seem very meagre and basic, limited to what could be grown personally or gleaned from the hedgerows and woods (where permitted). No doubt there was much poaching, despite the severe penalties if caught. Poultry and pigs were widely kept, although there were restrictions dependent on the available grazing on the waste, on the number of cattle that a person might keep. Some of the larger estates were allowed the privilege of a dovecote for breeding pigeons, but this was controlled because of the tendency of the foraging birds to raid other peoples' crops. However, all wild birds were fair game for those who could catch them. Bees were vital for providing the only form of artificial sweetening through their honey, although by the 1680s imported sugar loaves were beginning to appear at Houghton House.

For centuries it was the rule of the church that everyone should abstain from meat on Fridays and certain other days of fasting. The custom of eating only fish on Fridays became common practice in this country and continued long after the church's break with Rome. Fresh sea fish was out of the question in Bedfordshire, although salted fish was available and coarse fish were bred and kept in the local ponds. There were several fish ponds in the parks at this time, some, like Westminster pond (sometimes called Ware or Warren Lane pond) of great antiquity. Others mentioned in the 1680s were Swan bank pond, Marston Laune pond, and in Houghton Park the Upper Decoy pond, where wild ducks were trapped for the table. The Red Hart had its own pond in the Hop Ground (still there in Mr Nourish's garden), and in 1562 Thomas Middleton's will mentioned his 'little stew for fysh' in his garden in what is now Rectory Lane.[31]

The Houghton House accounts in the 1680s record routine purchases of rabbits (7s 6d a dozen), fowl, pigeons, plovers, sheep, beef, and fish. There were currants at Christmas, and salmon, anchovies, oysters, and 'pies from the French cook'. At other times, hogs, hams of Westphalia, and bacon. (The traditional English breakfast was already established, for the expenses of a journey to Sunning included a charge for 'bread, beer, eggs, bacon for all the company'.) Amongst the more exotic purchases were 'preserved lemons', 'excise fruit (i.e. subject to duty) and oranges from Spain', bamboo pickles, mangoes, dried fruit, green ginger' and a great quantity of chocolate (to drink). In 1676 '3lb of Chocolate for my Lord' (who had his own favourite chocolate pot) cost

18s.0d, and although in 1661 Lady Devonshire had written to her nephew Robert Bruce 'Tell my brother Tey is now highly in request' he seems to have stuck with his old favourite.

Tea would not become a common beverage until long after the period of this study. For most people Ampthill water was adequate enough refreshment so long as it was taken from the right springs or wells. The three main inns and owners of the larger houses brewed their own beer at this time, and the town housed several maltsters who supplied basic ingredients. Small beer (watered down) was a common drink for all ages. Imported wines were available to those who could afford them and fragments of the bottles the more expensive vintages came in can still be found from time to time. What would nowadays be known as home made wines were popular and can be found in recipe books of this period. Mead, a traditional drink since Saxon times and made from honey, was still made and drunk. The traditional Bedfordshire Clanger (meat one end, jam the other) had probably not yet come into its own, but Kattern Cakes baked in honour of Queen Katherine of Aragon, were well established. (Recipes Appendix C 3.)

The Feoffees
For centuries the needs of the community in education and the care of the sick and the poor had been attended to by the monasteries. But after the monasteries were dissolved the responsibility fell on the parishes. From 1572 it was possible to raise money for supporting the poor and needy through a rate, and from 1598 parish overseers were appointed by the magistrates with the authority to set the unemployed to work, those unwilling to co-operate being termed 'vagabonds'. Parliament passed a Poor Law Act in 1601 which was the legislation covering the period of this study. (Henry Webb is the first overseer of the poor to have been identified as yet in the 17th century, although there were doubtless many before him.)

Relief of the needy had always been a charitable obligation, and by the 17th century Ampthill had a long established trust regulated by trustees properly called Feoffees (pronounced *fee-fees*). Their income came from the management of property left to them over the years by wealthy inhabitants, to be used for the benefit of the town's destitute, and at this period the poor of Maulden. By the time covered by this study the Feoffees owned several acres of farm land and some properties in the town which they rented out. Buildings retained to provide free accommodation were known as Town Houses, or almshouses. A former Town House in the Kings Arms still bears a plaster roundel with crown, fleur-de-lys, the date 1677 and the initials W. H. thought to stand for Work House (as some Town Houses became at this time). Town Houses in Church Square remain in use, and although the earliest of the deeds to survive is dated 1485, the building's association with the Feoffees must go back very much further.

By 1623 the management of the Feoffee estate was haphazard and inefficient so three local Justices of the Peace, Sir Oliver Luke MP, Sir Edmund Conquest and Sir William Plummer, applied to Sir Humphrey Winch 'one of the Judges in the Court of Common Pleas at Westminster' (and also of Northill and Everton) for guidance. Sir Humphrey drew up a set of Orders (probably the first ever) for the estate's management. The churchwardens and overseers were to meet at least once a month on a Sunday, in church after Evening Prayer 'calling to them six or any four of the best subsidy men (ratepayers) with the parson for the time being (Hugh Reeve) . . . who shall set down and give directions how those moneys in stock shall be disposed of'. Leases and rents were to be paid half yearly – which suggests previous irregularity. In those pre-banking days the money would have been locked away in the Town Chest in the church (see Chapter 5).[32]

There are numerous examples of bequests to the poor in the wills of this time. In 1610 Elizabeth Newman left two pence for the poor 'to be expended at my buriall'. Jeffrey Palmer of the Red Hart, gentleman, wanted £5 to be divided amongst 'parishioners of the better sort' in 1619, and in the following year Alice Warner alias Waters, widow, left ten shillings 'unto the pore Widdowes . . . certaine pore Widows shall

have my wearing apparrell distributed between them'. In 1643 John
Stickley, yeoman, left to '20 of the poorest . . . 2 shillings A howse to the
people of the howse'.

High Days and Holy Days

In the old days major events in the church's calendar were marked as
Holy Days (holidays) and so long as church attendance was included,
the day could be spent in celebration and relaxation, vigorous for the
young, entertaining for the not so – until the puritans put a stop to all
such frivolity. The early Christians in England had taken over existing
pagan celebration dates and given them a new significance, but the original
impetus and outward symbolism, usually fertility rites — dancing,
(including Morris dancing) feasting and bonfires, remained. Christmas
and Easter are more obvious examples of old celebrations being taken
over, but sometimes the church initiated its own.

Mothering Sunday

It was usual for apprentices and young people living away from home in
service, to be given time off on Mid Lent Sunday (three weeks before
Easter Day) to go home and visit their mothers. Consequently one of
the names for this day is Mothering Sunday, partly because of the family
gathering but also as a reminder that all went on that day to their home
(or mother) church and to identify a key verse from one of the New
Testament readings set for the day – Saint Paul at his most abstruse on
the 'Jerusalem which is above is free; which is the mother of us all' –
Galatians iv verse 21.

May Day

May Day was less easy to 'convert' and while being Saint Phillip and
Saint James' day, the old celebrations were allowed to continue and
were at first often paid for by the church. It is not known where
Ampthill's maypole stood, but it is sure to have had one. Perhaps it was
in the town centre near the Market Cross? A more likely site was on
the waste in Slutts End, later known as the Sands, in front of the Alameda
gates. The Houghton House account books for the latter part of the 17th

century have references to 'Livery stockins' at Christmas and May Day, and in another year on the same occasions '10 Livery hats' whatever they were. In 1680 the milkmaids were given two shillings on May Day, whether each or between them is not clear.

Four years later 2s.6d. was given to 'the milkmaids with their garland' on 24th June, Midsummer Day, a pagan festival rededicated to mark the Nativity of Saint John the Baptist. Houses were then decorated with flowers and branches from trees 'to make good the Scripture prophecy respecting the Baptist, that many should rejoice at his birth. This custom was universal in England till the recent change in manners' commented a 19th century writer. May Day and Saint Valentine's Day songs survive in 19th century versions for Millbrook but surely date from much earlier times and would have been widely used in the district.[33]

Rogationtide
The word rogation comes from the Latin *rogatus* – to request, as in prayer, and the Rogation Days in the church's calendar are the Monday, Tuesday and Wednesday before Ascension Day, when it was customary to walk the parish boundary, and 'beat the bounds'. Along the route were clearly defined and carefully maintained boundary marks, such as a particular tree or prominent stone, or quite often a cross cut in the ground or built up in turf, where prayers would be said for the growing crops. (In Ampthill this was known as 'the Perambulation', and records survive from 1709.) At each stopping point it was sometimes the custom to impress the position of the marker on the memory of small boys by beating them or standing them on their heads! Occasionally there were disputes with inhabitants of neighbouring parishes engaged on the same task, as in 1712 when the Flitwick people tried, unsuccessfully, to claim part of Burridge's Field from the Steppingley men. Later a formal agreement was drawn up and signed, with a copy being written in the latter's parish register.[34]

Two customs which continued in Ampthill into the 19th century must have origins much further back in history. On 21st December, 'Doubting'

Saint Thomas's day, widows used to go round the town begging, or 'Goodening' as it was called. In the 1860s children from the National School in Bedford Street had the same aim in mind on Oak Apple Day, 29th May (King Charles II's birthday and the commemoration of his escape by hiding in an oak tree at Boscobel after the battle of Worcester in 1651) when they walked the streets chanting:

> *Hooray! Hooray! The 29th of May.*
> *If you don't give us a holiday,*
> *We will all run away.*

In return for money the donor would be given a sprig of oak to put in their buttonhole. It is possible the children had taken over a custom from apprentice boys and youngsters of earlier generations.[35]

Fun and Games
People of earlier generations were better at amusing themselves, at no cost and with minimum equipment, than in the present day. But it is rare for a game however ancient to be mentioned in local records, unless it is by way of evidence in court cases or proscription in codes of conduct. Inns, as always, would be patronized by customers playing tables (draughts), dice, cards and 'other unlawful games' unspecified but forbidden the clergy under canon law (Appendix C). John Jones was calmly 'att the signe of the Crowne takeinge of A pipe of tobacoe' in 1668 when he was arrested for theft. There was provision for billiards at Houghton House and outdoors a bowling green (there had been a bowling alley at Great Lodge probably from Henry VIII's day but reconstructed in Edward VI's time).

Archery was very popular, and young men had long been expected to practice in the churchyard after attending church. (King James issued a *Book of Sports,* to be read out in church, encouraging games after the service – much to the dismay of the puritans who were trying to impose Jewish Sabbath laws on to the Christian Sunday.) No doubt tipcat, the game John Bunyan was playing when he became aware of more

important matters, was played in Ampthill as well as in Elstow. Back in
1502 some Ampthill lads had been fined for playing 'lez bowles' and
'tenecias' when they shouldn't have been. 'Tenecias' may have been a
form of Real Tennis, but other bat and ball games are unlikely to have
borne much similarity to present day's major sports.[36]

Hunting, fishing, hawking, larking and other sports involving animals are
ubiquitous, but cock fighting on Boxing Day was a major event in the
Ampthill calendar. In 1680 John Newland broke into a house while the
family was in church on Christmas Day and stole £6 from a trunk so
that he could bet at the 'Great Cocking' the next day. There were cock
pens at Houghton House, and in 1688 Mr John Gaspar, Lord Ailesbury's
Gentleman of Horse, was given £1.10s – presumably for betting – when
he took James Bruce to the cockpit. A few years later Thomas
Underwood was keeping the cocks and received 8s.0d. whether as a tip
or in full payment of wages is not clear.[37]

Fire!
There was a constant fear of fire in the 17th century particularly in
settlements where thatched houses with wattle and daub walls were
packed tightly together. London's spectacular destruction in 1666 led to
some efforts being made at prevention and fire-fighting. (The Ampthill
Hospital built in Little Park in 1702 at the bequest of John Cross still has
its leather fire buckets.) Most towns had their own Great Fire at this
period, Ampthill's was in about 1676 when ten cottages belonging to
manor on the warren were amongst those destroyed.   A national appeal
through what were known as briefs – pleas for financial assistance read
out in all churches – was issued in 1679/80 with an estimate of the cost
of the damage being £469.7s. [38]

Morale
It is surprising how much is known of the ordinary and 'unimportant'
Ampthill people of the 17th century. But although we know their names
they remain faceless. We know of their work, family situations and
possessions, and hear of their troubles and tragedies more often than the

happy occasions probably because there were more of them. Their everyday language was that of the Authorized Version of the Bible, the *Book of Common Prayer*, and above all John Bunyan. (It is unlikely that any of the ordinary townsfolk would have heard of William Shakespeare, whose *Henry VIII* - which mentions Ampthill – was first acted in 1613, three years before his death.) But we can only judge the inner feelings of these people by measuring them against our own, and what in the 17th century might be the epitome of luxury and high living would today be anything but. Acceptable standards of behaviour between the classes were clearly defined in the Catechism in the *Book of Common Prayer* which all were supposed to know by heart. 'My duetie towards my neighboure is . . . To ordre myselfe lowly and reuerently to al my betters . . . to learne and labour truly to geate myne owne liuing, and to do my duetie in that state of lyfe, unto which it shall please god to call me'. In the opposite direction was the long Christian tradition of responsibility for the needy which was maintained locally in the 17th century by the Bruces at Houghton House, and by charitable bequests in the wills of ordinary townsfolk.

Hunger and sickness, and in the winter months cold and damp living conditions, would have been accepted as inevitable, and the smells generated by the presence of unwashed bodies and clothing and the absence of any drainage were considered normal. The manor court tried to control hygiene to acceptable standards of the day where it could, and the butchers who let their offal rot in the town pond, the Oxflood (site of Oxlet car park) were ordered to clear things up from time to time. And the stream which ran (and still runs) from Park Hill across the town centre and down the Red Hart yard was always little more than an open sewer. Even so, Ampthill seems to have avoided outbreaks of plague and serious epidemics at this time and retained its reputation as a very healthy place until well into the 20th century.

For most ordinary people fear was an ever-present emotion in their daily life. The fear of hell and purgatory lingered on from the middle ages supplemented by the 'fear of the Lord' and the fear of his wrath and vengeance promised in the Bible to those who didn't keep the Old Testament regulations as taught by the puritan preachers (and others). *Foxe's Book of Martyrs* with its lurid and gruesome tales of the Protestant sufferings of Bloody Mary's reign was officially endorsed by the bishops and widely read over many generations. Throughout the century there was constant fear of popish plots and take-overs – ever since Guy Fawkes and his friends tried to blow up parliament in 1605. 'A Form of Prayer and Thanksgiving . . . for the happy Deliverance of King James I and the Three Estates of England, [King, Lords, and Commons] from the most traiterous and bloody intended Massacre by Gunpowder . . .' on 5th November, 1605, was attached to *The Book of Common Prayer* until 1859.

There was fear associated with the religious/civil war being fought around the country. It is difficult to understand what it was like to have no reliable sources of information, when the only news was often gossip passed on in garbled versions. This fear of the unknown could often lead to panic, as Lord Ailesbury recalled in his memoirs of an incident following the flight of King James II in 1688: 'At Ampthill towne, near my house, the alarum was the same & the Inhabitants baricaded the . . . entrances into the Town by overthrowing carts. And messengers on horseback came crying out from Bedford, Luton, Dunstable & Owburne, that these towns were all set on fire by the Irish Papists & people were soe senseless & affrighted that they could not perceive that there was no fire in the Air for the farthest (*sic* – nearest) of those towns was but 8 milles from Ampthill . . .' [39]

Civil War

Forty years earlier, with civil war in progress, Ampthill people must have been similarly distressed, for whatever attitude the ordinary townsfolk adopted to the troubles, they could not escape them, and the future was unknown. There were no major battles in Bedfordshire, which was regarded as one of the staunchest counties in the parliamentary cause, but it would have supplied troops, horses and general support for both sides. Some, such as the innkeepers, might prosper as a result of increased passing trade, but others risked losing crops and stock to troops as they moved about the countryside. There were many complaints at the behaviour of parliamentary troops in this area in particular, and after the war was over it was estimated that the damage they had done in the county would cost £50,000 to put right.

Ampthill Raided

In 1643 the main action of the war was in the west country and in Scotland, but there was great excitement in Ampthill. The previous year parliament had introduced associations of counties 'for the mutual defence and safety of each other', and Bedfordshire was one of eight counties in the Midland Association, each county having its own committee. In October 1643 the Bedfordshire committee was meeting in Ampthill when a party of about 400 horse under the command of Sir Lewis Dyve raided the town. The troop had disguised themselves in the colours of the Earl of Essex, captain general of the parliamentary forces, which would easily be done before formal uniforms were in use, and so were not suspected. 'What distractions it caused in the Town may easily be imagined: all the Committee escaped but two whom they carried away prisoners, and Captain Temple, a valiant young Gentleman, who made good the gate of the Inne . . . yet was himselfe afterwards taken, stript to his shirt, and carried away prisoner. . . . The enemy staid not an hour in Ampthill, and took away with them the Country men's horses that were in the Towne'.[40]

The chaos caused by this incursion must have been considerable. Humphrey Iremonger, who lived in Church Square – his house survives in the core of Dynevor House – was an ardent royalist, and took advantage of the confusion to hurl abuse at the parliamentarians whom he threatened to hang outside his front door. Later he was with Sir Lewis Dyve and Prince Rupert at the occupation of Bedford and he was with the royalist forces at the battle of Towcester. His son William became a quartermaster in the royal army. The committee met again in Ampthill in 1644 ordering troops to muster in the town for the battle of Newbury, for which five horses were to be provided by the townsfolk.[41]

That year the king, who was staying at Woburn (his garrison was in Buckingham) proposed a muster in the heart of enemy country at Bedford. In the 28 miles between the two county towns were the parliamentary garrisons at Aylesbury and Newport Pagnell which he avoided by making for Great Barford. From there he moved on to Bedford, where there was a fracas on the bridge, and so on to raid Luton, but the Newport garrison having been alerted, the cavalier troop made a dash for Oxford. A number of skirmishes are known to have taken place in the Woburn area at this time.[42]

It was probably incidents like these that provoked a defiant (and dangerous) display of patriotism in Ampthill that year. The Red Hart was at that time held on a lease from the crown by Thomas Bussey, and it must have been on his instruction that a huge wall painting of the badge of the Prince of Wales, surrounded by a border of English roses and Scottish thistles, with the initials C P (Charles, Prince) and the date 1646, was painted over the fireplace of the most prominent ground floor front room. Was this the inn where the committee had met at the time of the 1643 raid? Probably not.

The King at Ampthill
In 1647 the Scots handed Charles over to parliament in return for a £400,000 payment and it was decided he should be taken to Hampton Court. Towards the end of the journey he was allowed a day or two's rest at Great Lodge in Ampthill where 'not without some difficulty' the Earl of Bedford gained permission to visit. He 'found his Majesty going to the prayers usual before his dinner'. Not surprisingly, 'cheerefulness there was not much in the King's looks'. Dinner was served and the earl waited on his Majesty but was unable to say much because of the presence of the guards. Charles escaped from Hampton Court and fled to Carisbrooke Castle in the Isle of Wight where he had expected to be made welcome, but the governor thought otherwise and treated him as a prisoner.[43]

The Protectorate and Beyond

The establishment of the Commonwealth would have been received in Ampthill with mixed feelings from both extremes – expectation and trepidation in equal measure – but surely everybody was hoping for peace and stability in church and state. The presence of the parliamentary surveyors measuring and questioning and noting everything down in their precise and thorough report would have been a major subject of conversation, and tenants of the royal estate must have been very worried as to their future. Would they be allowed to stay, or would they be moved on? There would have been a great deal of uncertainty all round.

At Houghton House and Great Lodge, where the king and queen and their children were familiar friends and visitors, life continued, presumably in a subdued state of semi-mourning minus younger members of the family who had followed the royal family into exile on the continent. But in the parks and elsewhere on the estate everybody worked with the routine efficiency an agricultural enterprise demands, although it is difficult to see how people like Benjamin Rhodes (Chapter 7) squared their Presbyterian conscience with service to such loyal supporters of the Stuarts as the Bruces.

For most people in Ampthill the Restoration would have been received with great relief and no doubt much toasting of King Charles beneath his crest in the Red Hart. So Ampthill resumed its old routines, with its inhabitants stoically accepting the political difficulties the nation would face over the rest of the century.

The Feoffees' Town House in Church Square, 1990, by Ronald L.Holt.

5

Church Life

'I pray that you may live long and promote the Word of God.'
Letter from Prince Edward (later King Edward VI) at Ampthill,
to Archbishop Thomas Cranmer, 18th June, 1545

Ampthill's ancient parish church, dedicated back in Norman times to the glory of God and in honour of Saint Andrew, would have been a sorry sight at the beginning of the 17th century with the 15th century nave and the tower in need of repair. But the faithful rallied round – as they always do – and in his will in 1612 Thomas Arnold, yeoman, gave two shillings to repair the windows in the north aisle (he left 'Mr Reeve, Parsone' five times that amount – ten shillings). Jeffrey Palmer, gentleman, bequeathed 20s for the same purpose in 1619, while Thomas Kirby, maltster, left 2s 6d for unspecified repairs in 1623. Two of the windows in the north aisle are known to have been associated with Sir John Cornwall and his wife, the princess Elizabeth of Lancaster, and one was her memorial. The mid-15th century leading in these windows would by now be in need of renewal, and it is probably this weathering that did more to hasten their disappearance than the attentions of the commissioners sent out by parliament in the 1640s to destroy or deface pictures, statues and altars. However, the Tabernacle of Our Lady in the north aisle would have lost its statue in this assault. Later in the century Robert Earl of Ailesbury gave five pounds-worth of wood towards repairing the 'north side of the church'.[44]

The chancel, its upkeep entirely the responsibility of the rector, was in such a dilapidated state in 1617 that the churchwardens reported the parson to the Archdeacon's Court in an attempt to get something done – as did their predecessors in 1556 and successors in 1769. But it was difficult to know what the rector of the day *could* do, given the miserably poor income he received. The communion table of Hugh Reeve's day would have been moved down into the nave and so no longer be in the position of an altar.

By now the interior walls of the church would have been whitewashed to cover over the medieval wall paintings, and perhaps texts had been painted on them in places. Over the chancel arch, where once there would have been a great painting of the Last Judgement – the Doom – would be a representation of the royal arms, ordered to be set up in churches after the break with Rome. The medieval rood screen (minus its rood – cross) survived across the chancel arch until 1728 when it was dismantled to make way for a pulpit. But its canopy of honour in the roof remained, and most of the medieval angels survived - and still do.

The font used in Parson Reeve's time dated from the 1330s but was replaced in 1891, for no good reason, by the present one. Fortunately there are some fine drawings of the old font, which in the 17th century would have stood just inside the south door. Features of the church interior from earlier ages familiar to Parson Reeve's congregation, and which have survived to the present day, include the memorial brasses to William and the Lady Agnes Hicchecok (1450), John and Margaret Lodington (1485), and John and Elyn Barnard (1506) then almost certainly still set in the floor and marking the graves of those they commemorate. Sir Nicholas Harvey's altar tomb of 1532 (removed in the 19th century, only the brass survived) stood over his grave beneath the eastern-most window of the north aisle, his helmet and gauntlet still hanging from a bracket fixed to the wall above.

Little is known of the church's furnishings at this time. According to an undated note in the parish register, Thomas, Earl of Elgin had given a crimson velvet pulpit cloth and cushion. The note continues: 'Charles Duncomb gave a very handsome flaggon for the communion, Mrs Rebekah Archer relict [widow] of Dr [Timothy] Archer gave a very good damask cloath and a couple of napkins of the same for the use of the communion, and Mr John Watson [of Little Park, son of the recusant] gave a couple of fair plates for the same use.' Sometime in the 1660s, Robert, Earl of Ailesbury provided wood to rail in the communion table, which would make it easier for the communicants to receive the sacrament kneeling, as the prayer book directed. (Archbishop Laud had insisted on communion rails thirty years earlier.) This was probably all part of the same post-Restoration refurbishment when a new bell inscribed 'Christopher Graye made me 1665' was installed.

The medieval lych gate 'tumbled down' in the 1720s but seems to have been relatively upright in the 1620s. Between the gate and the porch was the churchyard cross, perhaps in the position now occupied by the war memorial. The cross shaft incorporated carved scenes from the life of Christ, its remaining fragments now built into a credence table at the Lady Altar. The churchyard, in use since at least the 11th century, extended only a short distance into the present one. Somewhere north of the church stood the parsonage, burnt down in the late 1630s (see Chapter 8). In ancient times the main footpath to Houghton Conquest passed through the churchyard at the east end of the church.

Parish Officers
The Churchwardens, who were the sole representatives of the laity in the parish, filled an honourable office that stretched back to medieval times. Two parishioners were selected at the annual meeting, the Easter Vestry, to look after church finance and the upkeep of the building and its furnishings (except for the chancel, which was the rector's financial responsibility). At the same time the canons called for 'two or three or more discreet persons . . . to be chosen for Sidesmen' to assist the churchwardens. It was their responsibility to 'diligently see that all the parishioners duly resort to their Church upon all Sundays and Holy-days, and there continue the whole time of Divine Service; and none to walk or to stand idle or talking in the Church, or in the Church-yard, or in the Church-porch, during that time. And all such as shall be found slack or negligent . . . after due monition (if they amend not) they shall present

them to the Ordinary' i.e. Bishop, which in Ampthill meant the Archdeacon, who held a court to which offenders were summoned.

Very important was the Parish Clerk, appointed by the Minister and paid by the parish. He must be 'of twenty years of age at the least . . . of honest conversation, and sufficient for his reading, writing, and also for his competent skill in singing, if it may be'. It was his job to make the responses in the services in a loud voice, using the parish copy of the Book of Common Prayer on behalf of the congregation. Increasingly, as parish choirs came into existence, the clerk would be in charge of the music. Ampthill's parish clerks of the 17th century (unlike their successors) have not left much trace of their time in office. A note in the parish register covering 1669 to 1705 says 'William Paine put en Clarke of Ampthill Church June the 16', the year 1696 being given at the head of the previous page. An earlier hand lists gifts to the church from the Bruces and others so was perhaps the recipient of the payment noted in their 1684 household accounts 'Ampthill Clarks wages for a year 0-5-0' – a five shilling contribution from the estate.[45]

Visitations
Shortly after Easter the archdeacon would hold what was called his visitation. This was usually at a central church in the locality where all the newly elected churchwardens would be summoned to appear for swearing-in by the archdeacon's official, or legal officer. They would take with them a report (called a presentment) of the condition of their parish church, a general summary of the past year's activities, and answers to any specific questions the archdeacon may have asked. The archdeacon would then deliver his charge – his instructions to the churchwardens for their coming term of office. Similarly, from time to time, usually every three years, the bishop of a diocese (or his representative or commissary) would hold a visitation where clergy came together to receive the bishop's instructions and to report on their parishes. There would also be opportunity for the presentation of offenders (clergy and lay) for offences under canon law. Episcopal visitations in Ampthill in the 1630s were significant nationally, as will be seen.

Trials and Tribulations

Before Hugh Reeve came to Ampthill he had been on the staff of Bishop William Chaderton of Lincoln (1597 to 1614) who had been succeeded by John Williams, courtier and ecclesiastical maverick, and ultimately, despite a spell in the Tower of London, Archbishop of York. Bishop Williams had been content to ignore much that went on in his vast diocese and so when William Laud became Archbishop of Canterbury in 1633 and proposed conducting visitations of all the dioceses in his province, he started with Lincoln.

The visitation was carried out by his vicar-general Sir Nathaniel Brent, assisted by two commissioners, at four centres of which Ampthill was one. Two local agents were appointed, the vicar of Leighton Buzzard, Christopher Slater, and the rector of Ampthill, Hugh Reeve. The agents were to enquire on the condition of the church building, whether any church property had been unlawfully taken over, the conduct of clergy and laity and the extent of non-conformity in the parish. No detailed record of the visitation survives, although the vicar general probably summed the whole exercise up in a note: 'The countrie much complayneth of the court . . . Much complayning but noe prooving'.

The following year Bishop Williams carried out his own visitation. Dramatic repercussions followed. Two sermons (scholarly lectures for a private gathering of theologians – not routine Sunday discourses) which were preached on the occasion were subsequently printed, giving great offence to the puritans. In 1641 parliament ordered that copies should be burned in public by the common hangman in London and at the two universities.

Sunday no Sabbath

The greater offence was caused by the sermon *Sunday No Sabbath*, preached on 17th August 1635 by John Pocklington, Doctor of Divinity, chaplain to Charles I and the bishop of Lincoln, rector of Yielden and a magistrate.   The subject of the sermon, a sore one at the time, was whether Sunday, being the first day of the week and the Christian holy day, should have applied to it all the regulations the Old Testament decreed for the Jewish Sabbath – the seventh day of the week. Strict puritans said it should, others (supported by King James's *Book of Sports* which encouraged those who had attended church to spend the rest of the day in recreation) said that it shouldn't. The printed version of the sermon is 46 pages long, and it probably took at least two hours to preach. A typical extract reads:

'True it is, that some with great zeale and little judgement exclaime against recreations, and dressing of meat, and the like, on Sundaies must make a Sabbath of Sunday, & keepe up that name, otherwise their many citations of Scripture, mentioning onely the Sabbath, being applied to Sunday, will appear so ridiculously distorted and wry-neckt, that they will be a scorne and derision to the simplest of their now deluded Auditors . . . Hence it is that for some for want of wit [intelligence], some for too much, adore the Sabbath as an Image dropt downe from Jupiter, and cry before it, as they did before the golden Calfe . . .'

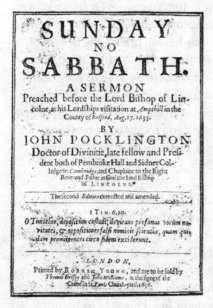 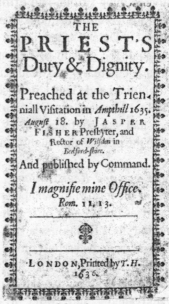

Title pages of the sermons in pamphlet form.

The following day a sermon entitled *The Priest's Duty & Dignity* was preached by Jasper Fisher, the Rector of Wilden, one-time divinity reader at Magdalen College Oxford (and a dramatist), on a text from Malachi 2.7: *'For the Priests lips should keepe knowledge, and they should seeke the Law at his Mouth: for he is the Messenger of the Lord of Hosts.'*. In print this ran to 54 (smaller) pages and is full of Latin and Greek quotations as well as classical references:

'My Argument, like my Auditory, is compounded of Priest and People: Both were now faulty, the Priest ignorant and lazie, the People unrulie and lawlesse; the unworthinesse of the first, and the ungodlinesse of the second, mutually producing, and mutually pardoning one another'. . . . 'Some will say we live in knowing times, and . . . though we are Pygmies in study and industry, yet exalted upon the antient Towres of Learning. By their helpe, we see farther then all fore-going ages; and we laugh at the dunsery of old Monks and Friers . . . Or consider the many present dissentions and controversies among Christians, which must needs be fathered upon Errour, and Errour upon Ignorance . . . Or looke downe upon the voluminous bookes of the Jesuites Societie, and the double harvest of Dutch Writers . . . For shall the benefit of Printing be revealed, and shall the growth of Learning be decayed? Shall Colledges and Libraries increase, and shall Knowledge decrease? Shall our studious Knighthood and Gentry flourish and fructifie in all kind of Science . . . Shall wee have so many incouragements from our Prince and Bishops, and shall wee confiscate all by an affected ignorance in teaching? . . . when the priest is thoroughly qualified, hee may be safely consulted . . .'

Registers and Registration
One of the most significant responsibilities placed on the church by the state was the keeping of registers for recording christenings, weddings and burials – functions carried out by the clergy for obvious religious reasons from the earliest times. In 1538 Thomas Cromwell, at the time Lord Great Chamberlain – and no stranger to Ampthill – ordered every parish to provide register books in which the information would be written weekly, and a 'sure coffer' to keep them in. This was to be provided

with two (later three) different locks, one for the parson, the other(s) for
the churchwardens, so that to avoid any 'misunderstandings' all three
should be present when the chest was opened.

Ampthill's chest, now set against the north door, is an 18th century
remodelling of an earlier version, as a peep at the back will confirm.
Lined with metal, presumably as a security/anti-fire precaution, it no
longer contains anything of value. Very few parishes still possess their
earliest registers, or indeed a complete run before the 18th century.
Ampthill's oldest surviving register covers the years 1604 to 1641, Parson
Reeve's time. and is significant as the last to record information relating
to the *whole* parish, before the establishment of non-conformist
denominations. From the early 1600s parishes were required to send a
copy of all their register entries to the bishop once a year. These copies
are known as Bishop's Transcripts (BTs) which quite often provide the
sole record for years where the registers are missing or damaged.
Because of the size of the Lincoln diocese, a second set of transcripts
had to be sent to the Archdeacon, so that there is usually a complete
series of names from about 1602 until the early 1640s.[46]

Commonwealth Arrangements
There is no record of baptisms, marriages or burials in the Ampthill
registers between 1641 and 1653. When parliament abolished the Prayer
Book in 1645 it ordered parishes to keep registers as before, but such
was the chaos of the time that few complied, and fewer books have
survived. By an act of 1653 the custody of the registers was taken
away from the minister who also lost the right to conduct marriage
ceremonies. A new secular official called the Parish Register (not
registrar), elected by ratepayers and sworn in by a magistrate, was to
keep the records. Marriages, after the calling of banns on three occasions
either in church or at the market place, were conducted by a magistrate.[47]

On the first page of Ampthill's second parish register is written:
'Bedd:[fordshire] By vertue of an Act of Parliament for the Regesteringe
of Births and Burialls and allsoe touchninge Marrigges and the

Regestering thereof we the inhabitants of Ampthill in the County aforesaid have made choyse of Robert Clearke of our said Towne to be Regester and is aproved by us whose names are hereunto subscribed Justices of the peace for the County afforesaid according to the said Act of Parliament in that case made and provided datted this 14 day of Aprill: 1654 [signatures of] John Okey, John Crook, Edmund Wingate.'

The register, in Robert Clarke's writing until December 1657, records births and burials usually with occupation or status and place of residence. Of particular interest are the details of 68 marriages which took place between between 1653 and 1658. Thirty couples came from elsewhere in the county, of the remainder at least one partner came from Ampthill. Of those, 30 had their banns called in the market place, the remaining eight specifying a church publication. The register entries are unusually full of family detail and in the case of the following examples, drama:

'WILLIAM HOLLIS of this parish of Ampthill in the Countye of Bedd: labourer, sonne of Elexander Hollis of the sayd towne, tayller, of the one partye, and GRACE PERSON of this parish spinster, servant to Christopher Whitemore maulter, daughter of Robert Person of parish Shittleington in the aforesayd County, weaver, of the other partye, was both heare present before mee the 26th day of April in the yeare 1654, and then they both entered their names into the booke that they were fully agreed upon marryage and that this their consent should be publyshed in the publique Markett place of Ampthill, first one April 27th 1654.'
'FRANCIS SMITH of parish Eversholt in the County of Bedd: widow, came the 28th day of April 1654, and then entered her name in the booke and doth absolutely forbidd nullyfye and make voyde all proceedeings in marryage which the afore named WILLYAM HOLLIS may or can have with any other partye without the License and leave of the afore named FRANCIS SMITH, widow.'

And five entries later: 'WILLYAM HOLLIS of this parish of Ampthill labourer, sonne of Elexander Hollis of this parish of Ampthill, tayler (of the one party) and FRANCIS SMITH of Eversholt, widow, are fully

consented and agreed upon marryagge, and they came both before mee
the 18th day of August and then entered their names for the publycation
in the parish Church of Ampthilll, first one July the ninth 1654, secondly
one July the 16th 1654, thirdly one July the 23 1654, being Sunday. The
certyficate given under hand Septr: 5th 1654, the above named partyes
was marryed before Justice Cooke [sic – John Crook] Sept: 5th 1654.'

An Intruded Minister
In 1641 King Charles gave way to parliamentary pressure to replace
Ampthill's rector Hugh Reeve with a minister whose teaching was more
acceptable to the puritan ideal and presented John Howe. Some would
have approved thoroughly, others would not, while many who did not
accept Parson Reeve's teaching would have been distressed at the
treatment he had received at the hands of those who wanted to get rid
of him.   Charles probably gave little thought to Ampthill as he signed
the deed of presentation for an 'intruded minister' having much weightier
worries to contend with.

The Directory
In 1645 parliament made the use of the prayer book illegal and in its
place ordered use of *A Directory for the Publique Worship of God,
Throughout the Three Kingdoms of England, Scotland, and Ireland*
which had been drawn up by under parliament's direction and would
form the basis for worship in Ampthill church (as elsewhere in the country)
for the next fifteen years. The *Directory* was not a book of set prayers
and planned services, but a manual of instruction for those who were to
lead worship. There is great emphasis on prayer and preaching, and the
Communion service was planned to exclude any suggestion of catholic
doctrine. The communicants are to sit at or round the table, and Jesus'
words of institution are read as 'a lesson of edification' instead of 'a
memorial before God'.

The whole of Sunday is to be celebrated as holy to the Lord, and total
abstinence is ordered not only from all sports and pastimes but also from
all worldly goods and thoughts. The directions for burial of the dead are

particularly harsh. The body is to be taken straight from the house to the grave 'and there immediately interred, without any Ceremony'. Prayers by the bereaved 'are Superstitious . . . therefore let all such things be laid aside.' However, friends should 'apply themselves to meditations, and conferences suitable to the occasion: and that the Minister . . . if he be present, may put them in remembrance of their duty.'

Farewell to Christmas
'Festivall daies, vulgarly called Holy daies, having no warrant in the Word of God, are not to be continued,' orders the *Directory*. (And that included Christmas Day, of course.) 'Publique solemne Fasting (which is to continue the whole Day) is a Duty that God expecteth' and means total abstinence 'from all food (unlese bodily weakness doe manifestly disable from holding out . . . in which case somewhat may be taken, yet very sparingly . . . when ready to faint).' Abstinence '. . . from all worldly labour, discourses and thoughts, and from all bodily delights (although at other times lawful) rich apparell, ornaments . . . garish attire, lascivious habits and gestures, and other vanities of either sexe' would be strictly enforced.

On the other hand, 'Dayes of Publique Thankesgiving' are to begin with the Minister making 'some pithy narration of the deliverance obtained' after which 'because singing of Psalmes is of all other the most proper Ordinance for expressing of Joy and Thanksgiving, let some pertinent Psalme be sung'. Following lengthy prayer and doubtless a much longer sermon, the Minister is to dismiss the congregation, but first he is 'solemnly to admonish them, to beware of all excesse and riot, tending to gluttony or drunkennesse . . . and to take care that their mirth and rejoycing be not carnall, but spirituall . . . and they themselves humble and sober . . . more cheerfull and inlarged further to celebrate his Praises in the midst of the Congregation, when they return unto it, in the remaining part of the Day.'

Restoration

Life under the Lord Protector must have been depressing and gloomy
for those without strong puritan convictions or a gift to experience and
appreciate 'spirituall mirth'. The restoration of the monarchy brought
with it a return to the use of the prayer book and a conference
was called to consider its revision, but after four months of deliberation
ended in stalemate. Many of the puritans considered it sinful to teach
what the bishops considered it sinful not to teach, so the bishops set
about their own revision, and the new book was brought into use on 19th
May 1662. The question which had vexed the century, as to whether
the Church of England should be Presbyterian or not, was now firmly
settled.

Nonconformity

For the next 20 years every effort was made by parliament to enforce
conformity to the Church of England and to prevent the growth of
alternative religious groups yet despite legal proscription and powerful
opposition at local level they survived. There was still no concept of
freedom of worship as we understand it. Fines and other penalties
were imposed on those who were unable to conform, with imprisonment
for leaders and unlicensed preachers like John Bunyan, who with their
followers suffered intolerable local persecution and ridicule. Nobody
could hold any public office, attend the universities or similar institutions,
or serve in the army unless they received the sacrament in the Church
of England. It was not until 1689, at the beginning of the reign of William
and Mary, that there was freedom of worship for dissenters who were
willing to take the oath of allegiance, although they were still barred
from public office until 1828, Roman Catholics a year later.

*Overleaf, pages from the parish register for 1611 and 1612, in
Hugh Reeve's handwriting. The first entry (top left) records the burial
of his son Richard Reeve (born 1607) on 22nd July. The signatures
of the rector and his churchwardens, Peter Martin and Thomas
Kirbie, appear at the end of the year. (See page 117 note on the
calendar.)*

60

Richard Roebe the sonne
of Hugh Roeb was buried
the 22th of July

Scrithro Evans the daughter
of Richard Evans was baptiz
the 28th of July

Susan Foorman the
daughter of Richard Foor
man was baptized the
18th of August

Alce Darmud the daught
of Thomas Darmud was
baptized the 29th of Sept

John Harro?t was buried
the 5th of October

Sheffere Killingworth,
the sonne of Thomas
Killingworth was baptized
the 6th of October

Willm Smyth the sonne
of George Smyth was
baptized the 11 of Novem

William Emeston and
Elizabet Giblio wear
maried the 17th of Novem

John Hall the sonne of
Bartho: Hall was baptized
the first of December

William Provotte the sonne of
William Provotte was buried
the 7th of December

Priscila Knife the daughter
of Richard Knife and
Elizabeth

Elizabeth Smyth the daught
of John Smyth vicar was
baptized the 8th of Janu

the wife of Willm Oliver
was buried the 13th of
January

Elizabeth Bull the daughter
of John Bull was baptiz
the 26th of January

widow Reade was buried
the 30 of January

Thomas Abbat of London
Bara Conquest ugage?

Jerome Robines the ?
of Richard Robines

Marie Eton the daughter
of William Eton and
marie Squire the
daughter of John Squir
weare baptized the
16th of February

Joan Reade was buried
the 17th of February

William Harmor the sonne
of Francis Harmor was
baptizd the 23 February

Bartholmew Johnston was
buried the 7th of march

martin woodward the sonne
of Francis woodward was
baptizd the 15 of march

father Hill was buried
the 13th of march

Hugh Reede Rect.
peter martin Churw
Thomas Giblio wardens

Anno Dom 1612

John ?
of ? was
baptiz the 29th of
march

marie knotivell was
buried the 13 of Aprill

George Cuttro was buried
the 19th of Aprill

Anna Board the daughter
of William Board was baptiz
the first of June

John Owen and ? wall
weare maried the first of
June

? ? the sonne
of ?

6

Townsfolk

'*Some will say we live in knowing times, and . . . we see farther than all fore-going ages: [but] consider the many present dissentions and controversies among Christians . . .*'

Jasper Fisher, Rector of Wilden, in a sermon 'The Priest's Duty & Dignity,' preached in Ampthill Church, 18th August, 1635

It is likely that Ampthill's population through most of the 17th century was under 500. A visitation return of 1603 recorded 220 communicants at Easter, when *all* the town's adult population of 16 and over were supposed to communicate, indicating a lower figure at the beginning of the century as might be expected. But a survey of the religious affiliation of inhabitants over the age of 16 made in 1676, with the town prospering as a result of the Bruces being at Houghton House, suggests a population of about 550. The total number of ceremonies recorded in the earliest parish register to have survived supports this estimate. It covers the years 1602 to 1641 (with a few minor gaps) and the handwriting is Parson Reeve's.

Baptisms noted between 1602 and 1641 total 667 (335 boys, 332 girls) including two sets of twins, Francis and John Dowland in 1615 and Edward and Jane Crouch in 1628. The highest yearly birth rate with 34 baptisms – 17 boys, 17 girls, almost double the average, was 1624, with four baptisms in November, five in December, four in January and nine in February. There were 168 weddings in the parish, seven by licence (and a double one in 1617 when the Dowland sisters married). Deaths totalled 423, 128 of whom were children – if we assume that where a parent's name is given the burial is that of a child. For 21 of the 40 years recorded, the number of deaths did not reach double figures. The worst year during Parson Reeve's time was 1639, with 33 deaths (10 children) never more than five in any one month. (Which is only two less than the unhealthy year 1657 – see Chapter 7.) Most burials were evenly distributed through the year, so epidemics and plague seem to have been kept at bay (justifying the town's healthy reputation) unless the Grim Reaper struck in 1621 and 1622 when the registers are incomplete.[48]

Occupations

From the parish registers and other documentary sources more than thirty separate occupations have been identified for Ampthill people in this period – esquires and gentlemen excluded. There were butchers and bakers of course, but no candlestick maker. No doubt Thomas Murrill the blacksmith would have made many candlesticks in his time, and perhaps William Heady the carpenter, who became blind towards the end of his life, or Richard Exton a joiner. Hugh Smith was a potter who had his kilns on the corner of Bedford Street and Church Street in the early 1600s and at one time was a draper too. Lawrence Ebden was 'coallyer' for Lord Elgin – in those days coal for Houghton House, brought to Great Barford from Kings Lynn in barges, was purchased by the cauldron.

Thomas Lines was a glover in the 1620s when John Flawne was the shoemaker. William Underwood is one of the tailors mentioned at this time, and doubtless made up cloth woven by Thomas Blyth of Bedford Street. Richard Beech was a wool-winder, probably getting his wool from sheep looked after by shepherds Robert Silcocke and Henry Watson. William Stokes was one of several husbandmen – farmers – of the period, and John Kilby was a bricklayer who lived for a while in Maulden. (It is surprising how many of these family names can still be found in the neighbourhood.) Christopher Grey had a bell foundry in Ampthill for about nine years, and cast a bell here for Jesus College Cambridge in 1659. Most intriguing is Edward Harris 'late of Ampthill, but now resydent in London' who came back to the town to bury his son Thomas in 1655. He is described as a limner, which at this period would mean that he painted miniature portraits. In addition almost every household would have had lace makers amongst its members, from the youngest children to the oldest 'Goody'.[49]

Notoriety

It is an unfortunate fluke of history that most ordinary people are unlikely to be remembered by posterity unless they get on the wrong side of the law or leave interesting wills. Occasionally at this time the rector records in the parish register characters who would otherwise have passed totally into oblivion. What was the story behind the 'Twoe Straingers' buried on 29th and 30th December 1606? We don't even know their sex, let alone approximate age or cause of death. Did 'Beniamine a bastard' christened in 1624 survive infancy, and if so, what did he make of his life? And 'Old Richard' buried in 1636, what tales could he tell? Fortunately we know more about petty offenders who came before the manor court in the Moot Hall, and although the records for the early 1600s are missing, a court roll of 1587 records payments received by the court for offences which could equally have been committed at any time in the succeeding century when the names of some of the offenders recur in what must be their children or grandchildren.[50]

In 1587, for example, Thomas Wood and Richard Middleton, innkeepers, were fined 4d each for overcharging. Widow Beard, Clement Bayley (died 1618), John Piggott and four others were fined 4d each for being 'common tipplers'. Thomas Newbold, butcher (probably he who was buried in 1605) who sold 'unwholesome meat' was fined 6d, although his partner in crime John Lane only had to pay 4d. Richard Bell a baker, was fined heavily – 12d – for selling 'unwholesome bread', whilst his co-offender Thomas Pearce (surely the same who was churchwarden in 1615 and 1625) paid the usual 4d. It would be interesting to know more behind the crime of Thomas Beard, chandler, accused of 'deceit and fraud' which earned him a routine 4d fine: he was buried in 1605.

James Button, gentleman, member of a respected Ampthill family, had sub-let some of the property he held, without permission, and had been

ordered by a previous court to evict his tenant but hadn't, so was fined
3s.4d – as were William Lyffyn and Richard Cooke for the same offence.
Henry Allen had taken a lodger 'against the order' (accommodation of
strangers was strictly regulated as a precaution against having people
left on the rates as paupers) and he was fined 12d. John Tavernor had
cut down two trees in Ware (Warren) Lane (Millbrook road) without
permission and was fined 13s 4d. Edward Middleton and his wife
Dorothy had 'illegally recovered' their cattle from the bailiff – which
had probably been impounded for straying on the common – and were
fined ten shillings. Edward Fisher and Thomas Wood were described as
'common hunters' – poachers – and were let off with a fine of 12d
each.

Church Courts
Although always the subject of dispute, the scope of the church courts
(based on Canon Law) was clearly defined and separate from the king's
courts, the former having responsibility for religious and moral issues
including clergy discipline. It was the churchwardens' duty to present
offenders at the church court for trial and possible punishment. Quite
often this would involve excommunication, exclusion from the right to
receive the sacraments of the church, burial in the churchyard, and being
ostracised by family, friends and the community. Some of the records of
the Archdeacon of Bedford's court have survived, but for the period of
this work only the years 1616 to 1618 when it was convened 25 times,
all but four of those sessions being held at Ampthill. Later the court was
presided over by the Archdeacon's Commissary, usually in S.Paul's
Church, Bedford.[51]

Religious offences form the bulk of the court's cases in 1617/18. Amongst
the Ampthill offenders was Richard Robins summoned for being absent
from his parish church 'at Evening prayer by occasion of his going to
some neybour churches to hear a sermon' and taking his servant William
Glinister with him. He was warned 'to attend his parish church at Vespers
for six Sundays running' and presumably did so, as no more is heard of
the matter. Robins died in 1629, his widow Mary eleven years later. Her

interesting will is mentioned below. James Woodward (who rented a section of the Moot Hall and a property with adjoining field in Dunstable Street) was presented for the same offence as Richard Robins and for not communicating. He alleged 'he was rejected by Mr Reeve' the rector, who being present explained why. The court ordered him to receive and Mr Reeve to administer the Holy Communion, but a month later he had not complied. Edward Woodward, probably James's brother, had property on the east side of Church Square where Brandreth House is now, and in the town centre at what is now 7 Church Street. He was presented for not communicating and for 'railing and scoulding [horseplay – larking about] with Edward Defraine on the Sabothe day'. Both seem to have denied the charge and the case was dismissed. (Edward Woodward was churchwarden in 1640).

Elizabeth Raynard was charged with 'rayling [heckling] and striking the minister in church in time of divine service' in May 1617. She was summoned on two occasions but did not appear so was excommunicated. However, the matter was patched up and a certificate provided by the rector allowed the removal of her excommunication in July 1617. Similarly, William Savage, having been presented for not communicating, came with a certificate which cleared the way for his case to be dismissed.

The court also dealt with matters of morality. In 1617/18, for example, a man named Whitaker recounted a rumour that Alice Burwell had been made pregnant by Daniel Potter and both were presented on a charge of fornication. Potter denied the accusation, but Alice Burwell, who was 'accustomed to have sexual intercourses in the home' (as it was delicately put) and who had been summoned to appear, didn't. The case rumbled on over three court sessions, and Alice, who was excommunicated, is not heard of again.

A happier duty of the court was to investigate applications for marriage licences, and in April 1617 Thomas Hambleton paid the customary fee of 11s 4d to marry Emma Haskett of Hockliffe. The parish register records the baptism of Robert (1627) and Mary (1630) the children of

Thomas, and the burial of the latter in 1635. Perhaps 'Captaine' Hambleton, who was buried in 1625, was his father? Sometimes the archdeacon would appoint a deputy, or surrogate, to be responsible for dealing with marriage licences, and for thirty years, whilst rector of Ampthill, Hugh Reeve was the surrogate.

Treasured Possessions
Despite the solemnity of the occasion that surrounds the making of a will it is possible to gain an insight into the character of its maker especially when a variety of items are bequeathed and squabbling families must be satisfied. *The Book of Common Prayer* in the 1552 version Parson Reeve would have used has in 'The Ordre for the Visitacion of the Sicke' – a lengthy service – a rubric (instruction) requiring the Minister to 'examine whether he [the sick person] be in charitie with al the world: Exhorting him to forgeuve from the bottome of his hearte al persons that have offended hym: and yf he have offended others to aske them forgeuenesse . . . And yf he haue not afore disposed hys goodes, let hym then make his wyl . . .'

Occasionally a form of will known as nuncupative, or spoken, was allowed. This was a formal statement by witnesses of what the testator had said before death. Parson Reeve recorded the wishes of Henry Page, who died in 1624, interesting for being as short as a will could be 'I give all that I have to my wiffe' (see page 71). Another nuncupative will made in 1605 by Agnes Felce suggests conscience prompted by the prayer book rubric when she remembers her cousin Jeremy Wolfe 'for he is worthie of yt . . . for he hath been my good freend & deserved more than I gave'.

Most people seem to have been very close to death at the time of making their wills and reading from the original manuscripts after 400 years the pathos is sometimes still very real. Henry White, yeoman, of Bedford Street, dying on 27th June 1625, with Robert Woodcoke his 'Phisicion' standing by, dictated his instructions to Parson Reeve who was to receive ten shillings for writing the will. Robert Woodcocke was bequeathed 25 shillings and eightpence – presumably for professional services rendered – a good way of making sure the doctor's bill was paid. His wife Elizabeth was taken care of by 'statute' – the law that if a man's property was copyhold, the widow had a third for her lifetime. So after remembering friends and relatives, 'Gaberrell Munes and the boye my fellow servauntes' were given five shillings each, the former also inheriting the 'horne and the stringes'. A postscript gives five shillings to 'the goodwife Dearman my laundrie' woman. In 1639 James Bird had left 'Elizabeth Kellow my keeper in my sickness xxs', but Ellen Higgins 'lying sick upon hir bed' in 1646 when she made her will, survived another year before it was needed.

Clothes form a valuable part of a person's estate at this time. Henry White (above) had a 'Green Button suitt and a paire of greene stokins . . . a pair of greene garters . . a shirt and 2 bands' to bequeath. Ambrose Samm (1659) left his 'heare [hair] Coate' to his brother In 1604 William Younger, chapman (pedlar) had left 'all my other children which I had by my twoe former wives a dozen of silk poynts [ornamented part of stocking above the ankles] or vi pence in money'. The practical (and probably puritan) Elizabeth Newman left Mary Squire 'my ould gowne to make a coate for one of her children' in 1610.

Martha Hill and Mary Robins, who both died in the same year, 1639/40, took their religion seriously, the Robins family being puritan. (Mary's husband Richard had been in trouble for missing Vespers at Ampthill to hear sermons at Hawnes). The usual practice of the day was to begin a will 'In the name of God. Amen' and after identifying yourself and confirming that you were of sound mind, to bequeath your soul to God who gave it to you and your body for burial. Some took the opportunity to expand this into a little sermon, perhaps provided and prompted by the parson.

Martha Hill, a spinster in the original sense of a spinner of wool, cotton or hemp, leaves her 'soul to god that gave it me and by his mercy through Jesus Christ my alone Saviour hath redeemed it and by the fellowshippe of his holy spiritt hath kept it from manifold sins and iminent dangers during this my pilgrimage on this earth with the blessed Trinitie I doe beleeve shall and will by the all sufficient power thereof in the fullnesse of time reunite both soule and body and glorifie them that I may praise god in heaven eternally . . .as for the worldly goods which god hath lent me and through my friends love I doe possesse . . .'

She then divides amongst her friends and relations 'a greene sattin petticoate & waste coate trimed with silver bone lace [i.e. pillow lace, so called because the bobbins used in its making were often made of bone] . . . a redd sattin wastecoate trimed with silver lace . . .along white feather fixt with red . . a holland wastecoate, holland Aprone . . . a Holland handkerchief laced with nett-worke lace . . . a coife & a crosse cloathe wrought with red silke and set with boas [bows] . . . a Red bayes petticoate & wastecoate.'

Mary Robins on the other hand leaves her daughter Sarah '2 petticoats, 2 wastcoates, 2 smocks', daughter Elizabeth has 'a cloake a petticoate, a pair of whalebone bodies [bodices], while daughter Marie gets a 'black stuffe gowne . . .' Martha Hill has 'cushions of clothe of gold . . . and a Cushion cloathe with seaming lase' but doesn't mention any furniture. Each of the Robins children is sensibly set up, William with '2 joynt stooles & a basse [wicker] chair', Jeremy with a basse chair and a pot shelf, and while he gets the Bible, Sarah has the 'Great brasse kettle, one boulster, one pillow, one pair of sheets, 2 chests & all that is in them. Agnes has money and Elizabeth gets 'andirons, a warming pan, pewter candlestick, pewter dish, little kettle, brass morter with pestell'. Marie has 'a Feather bed, standing bedstead, blanket bolster, pillow, coverlet, wicker chair, porridge pot, dripping pan, fire shovel and a pair of tonges'.

Thomas Sandy, a turner who died in 1665, comes over as a pernickety old gentleman who didn't trust his wife to take care of her inheritance and suspected his family would be fighting over theirs. Nat Reynolds, his servant, was given a set of tools and 20 shillings, and Francis wife of William Hollis received five shillings 'for her care and paines she tooke

Plate 1

Houghton House north and west fronts. No contemporary colour picture of the house survives. Neither are there any pictures of the interior. Of the fixtures and fittings dispersed when the house was dismantled in 1794, the staircase is the most notable and best authenticated

See pages 5 and 6 for further notes on these pictures

Plate 2

Plate 3

House in Church Street, Ampthill, once Edmund Wingate's, now 31-35A. Exterior c 1890. Interior of 31 following restoration in 1994. (courtesy Mr Simon Houfe). Memorial in Meppershall church to Revd Timothy Archer, shown in his pulpit there. He owned the house from the 1670s.

Plate 4

Ampthill church's mediaeval font (1330s) would have been familiar to Parson Hugh Reeve.

Plate 5

Memorial to Richard Nicolls, born in Ampthill, who named New York, with the canon ball that killed him in 1672. The flags were added in the 1940s for the benefit of visiting American servicemen.

Plate 6

Wall painting, 1646, in the (then) Red Hart honouring Charles Prince of Wales, shortly to become King Charles II.
Pargetting roundel 'W.H. 1677' ('Work House') on the Town House in the King's Arms Yard. 1950s photograph.

Plate 7

Ewe Green, looking towards Flitwick in about 1820, the Grange farm on the right. Drainage of the Warren (on the left), following its enclosure in 1808, is in progress, but otherwise the scene is little changed from the 17th century.

The view from as close to the same position as possible, July 2000

Plate 8

Maulden Church, with the Bruce Mausoleum as constructed by Benjamin Rhodes

Conquest Bury, (Bury Farm marks its site today) the home of Richard Conquest's family. The Grange and the lodge in Little Park, would have been constructed in similar style.

with me in my sickness'. But his own wife Juliana was warned that the chattels she received were 'not to be imbezild', and to his daughter went 'my wives best red Pettycoate . . . immediately after my said wives decease'. Further, 'if any person or persons herein mention'd shall not acquiess & be content with their Legacies . . . then my will is That such person soe offended shall lose his or her or their Legacye and I give him or them only twelve pound . . .' Daughter Ann, wife of Richard Franks, had four years to wait for the red pettycoate, for Julyana the wife of Thomas Sandy was buried on 17th January 1669.

The items of furniture most frequently mentioned are stools, tables, cupboards and bedsteads, and every family would possess them in greater or lesser quantity (and quality) depending on their means. Isabell Pearce (1611) has a 'painted cheste' and Ambrose Samm (1659) passed on much loved objects 'our rounde Table . . . our old Cheare'. He had a 'Studdey' as had Henry Lucas who in 1616 gave 'all my books and my desk in my studie' to his son Caesar. 'I give my quearne [stone hand mill] & my powderinge troffe [for salting bacon] to him that shall have the howse by cause I will not have them removed,' requested Elizabeth Newman in 1610. Sometimes sheep or cattle are bequeathed, as in 1654 when Timothy Bayley, yeoman, left each of his grandchildren an 'Ewe tagg & weather Tagg' out of his Ampthill flocks. Parson Reeve left his Godson 6s 8d 'to buy him an Ewe lambe' in 1645.

The education of the deceased's children is often arranged. In 1615 Ann Smithson, widow, left £10 to Francis Cooper, victualler, for the education of her daughter Ann for five years, the first three 'att her booke and needle' and then 'to make bone [pillow] lace and to knitte'. Geoffrey Shortridge of the Crown wanted his son 'to bee brought up with good learning and all other conveniences' in 1656. Unfortunately Anne Bushby's parents were poor and made no provision for her education, but the Overseers of the Poor stepped in and apprenticed her to Thomas Rose, butcher, of Bedford, and his wife to learn 'spinninge, knittinge, & such like household Businesse'. That was in 1669.

Tools and equipment were highly valued, and Jeremy Pearce, yeoman, mentions his 'plowes, cartes, plowe timber, cart wheeles, harrowes, and all my implements of husbandry' including 'horses & horse harness . . .Timber & Bordes in the Yard . . .' He also has a 'fatt [vat], 2 boulting arkes, Troffes and all the moulding boards in the backhouse' – that was in 1625. In 1628 John Wiley, a cook, bequeaths his 'bruing vessell with Tubbs, payles, kinmilles' (more tubs). William Tomlinson, blacksmith, (1644) leaves his son William 'the Anfeld & belows in the shop and all the tolles in the shop', and in 1647 Ellen Higgins (presumably a spinster) left her servant 'Goody Wharlo one peece of woolen cloth and the bed she lyeth on all exceptting the matteris and the covorlid' and to 'Goody Baker three poundes of hempe'.

Family concerns are ever present. Wyllyam Watson, who died in 1605, had two children, Jeremy and Alice. Jeremy had obviously moved away and fallen out with his father so he received forty shillings, half of it a month after his father's death, the rest within a year. Daughter Alice married William Blythe (he died in 1633, she in 1638) and they had three daughters, Marie, Johane, and Elizabeth and a son Thomas (who grew up to feature in the Hugh Reeve story – see below). Each of the daughters received £5 from their grandfather 'not to be paid before the day of their mariage or at the age of xxvi' (26 – not the customary 21) and household goods to start them off in married life (they have to wait until then to inherit).

Marie's bequest included 'one Cupbord, a brasse pott, a great Ketteell, twoo pewter platters, one pewter dishe, a Candlestick, a salt seller . . . a table with a frame (i.e. trestle table) one stoole and a Cushion'. Johane had utensils including what looks like 'a shroddinge knife' (shredding? Shredding what?). Elizabeth received 'one bedsted, one flocke bedd, one fetherbed, a bolster . . . a pillowe, twoo pillowbeares (pillow cases) two blanketts, one coverlett . . . one blanket sowed together, twoo Coverlettes sowed together . . . twoo cushions, half a dozen of pewter spones, a great boole (bowl), a paire of bellowes and a paire of tonges.'

Grandson Thomas Blyth would inherit the adjoining properties in Bedford Street, but not until he 'accomplishe the age of one and twentie yeares or doe marrie', meanwhile he and his mother were to share the property 'wherein I now dwell'. But after Thomas reaches 21 or gains a wife, then Alice (his mother) is to live in one and Thomas (who is to pay his mother 'tenne shillinge everie yeare so longe as she liveth') in the other. After his mother's death he is to pay his sister Elizabeth vi shillings and viii pence a year 'so long as she liveth'. Also remembered by Wyllyam Watson was 'Oliver Brown the sonne of John Brown' who is to receive 'xx shillings at the age of twelve yeares if he live so longe.' (No Oliver Brown appears in the burial register!)

One townsman who really prospered was William Nashe, warrener, and a relative of the Conquests, who died in 1607. When Andrew Noone, warrener, had died in 1585, William had been his man servant and received a bequest of 20s and Noone's 'best fryce [frieze – coarse wool] cote, my blew cote, my buck leather hose'. A generation later, William Nashe's own will mentions Agnes Noone, widow, and her daughter Agnes, who is to receive £10 – a large sum of money compared with the usual legacies of the period, 'conditionally that she do marry with her mother's good likinge'. There are generous bequests to the Conquest family 'to be bestowed . . . in two several peeces of plate for them', Richard, son of Sir Edmund Conquest, is to receive the same, as are the children of John Neale, junior, gentleman. There are bequests to the poor of Ampthill, Houghton Conquest and Maulden and payments to the ringers of each of the three parishes.[52]

Part of probate copy of Henry Page's will (see page 66) which reads: 'The last Will & testament nuncupative of | Henry Page ^ late which then lived ^ of Ampthill in the County and | Archdeaconry of Bedford ^ deceased ^ by him made in his lyfe | tyme & after his death put into writeing as followeth. | Vizt [Videlicet – 'that is to say'] | The sayd deceased being of perfect mynde & memorie in the | presence of Hugh Reeve Clarke did about the seaventeenth of | ^ day ^ September Anno Dm 1624 Utter his mynde to the effect following | Vizt: | I give all that I have to my wyffe.' He was buried on 31st October, 1624.

7

Some Local Worthies

'Richard Nichols Esqr one of the Dk of Yorkes Bedchamber
was buryed June 11th'
Ampthill Parish Register entry, 1672

'*Richard Nichols Esqr one of the Dk of Yorkes Bedchamber
was buryed June 11th*'
Ampthill Parish Register entry, 1672

King Henry VIII is rightly credited with having brought Ampthill into prominence, but in the succeeding reigns of his three children the town fell into decline and decay. With the accession of James I, Ampthill came back to life, for he was as keen a sportsman as Henry had been and the parks needed properly managing after years of neglect. The new king appointed his childhood friend Thomas Erskine (by then Viscount Fenton) High Steward of the Honour and keeper of the parks and leased part of Dame Ellensbury Park to the Countess of Pembroke so that she could build Houghton House. Most significantly he appointed Lord Bruce to succeed Lord Fenton as High Steward of the Honour, so introducing a family who were to give outstanding service to the town and county over three generations, as will be seen.

Mary Herbert
Born in 1561, Mary Sidney was a niece of Robert Dudley, Earl of Leicester, favourite of Queen Elizabeth I. Her brother was Sir Philip Sidney, courtier, soldier, statesman musician, and poet, who died at Arnhem following the battle of Zutphen in 1586. John Aubrey, the 17th century antiquarian, gossip and biographer said of Mary Herbert 'She was a beautiful Ladie and had an excellent witt, and had the best breeding that that age could afford. She had a pritty sharpe-ovall face. Her haire was of a reddish yellowe.' A portrait of her dated 1614 and attributed to Marcus Gheeraedts bears a caption 'No Spring 'till now' a reference, it has been suggested, to her personality as much as her beauty.

Mary Sidney was well educated, translated French poetry, and collaborated with her brother Philip in writing a metrical version of the psalms. Later she revised and added to his poem *Arcadia*, the work for which he was most famous. She married Henry, Earl of Pembroke who died in 1601 to be succeeded by their son who was in the entourage of James I. Perhaps it was through her son that she came to know of Ampthill Castle? It was said that she tried to persuade James I to let her rebuild it, but he planned to do this himself and instead gave her a lease of Dame Ellensbury Park in 1615, where she built Houghton House. She died in 1621 barely six years after Houghton House was built, and was buried in Salisbury Cathedral. There is no monument to her there, but a much quoted epitaph by Ben Jonson with a second stanza by William Browne remembers 'the subject of all verse, Sydney's sister – Pembroke's mother'.[53]

The Bruces

When Queen Elizabeth I died in 1603 and her successor James VI of Scotland became also James I of England, the succession was smoother than it might have been, due to the diplomatic groundwork of Sir Edward Bruce, who had served as James's special envoy to the queen. Sir Edward accompanied the new king to England, was created Baron Bruce of Kinloss and appointed Master of the Rolls, a key judicial post. When he died in 1611, he was succeeded by his son - also Edward. Two years later the new baron challenged Sir Edward Sackville to a duel (in Holland) and was killed. His heart was removed, placed in a silver casket, and taken to Culross Abbey in Scotland for burial. Sir Edward's brother Thomas (1599-1663) succeeded to the title and in the same year was appointed by King James to succeed Lord Fenton as hereditary steward of the Ampthill honour charged with the preservation of game 'for the exercise of falconry and venery and fishing'. It is likely that Lord Bruce, who was created Earl of Elgin in 1633, and Baron Whorlton in 1641, lived at Great Lodge for a time, but from about 1620 the family home for three generations would be Houghton House.[54]

In 1644 the king summoned parliament to meet at Oxford. Lord Elgin, by then in his mid-forties, was not physically robust (a biographer says he was a hypochondriac) and preferred a quiet life with his second (and younger) wife at Houghton House. But he felt duty bound (if reluctant) to obey the king's summons and was pulling on his boots and ready to set out when his tearful wife threw herself at his feet and did her utmost to make him change his mind and stay at home. She drew grim pictures of what might happen to them and their estate if the parliamentarians won. 'Will you reduce me to *milk a cow*?' she pleaded. The earl took off his boots and stayed at home, his reputation in royal circles permanently damaged despite his support for those who were to suffer as the war progressed.   Lord Elgin was not alone in his lack of enthusiasm for the war, and there was much apathy towards fighting, and evasion of conscription and desertion was not unusual. [55]

Other members of the Bruce family who will appear in these pages include Robert (1627-1685), who succeeded his father as 2nd Earl of Elgin and was created Baron Bruce of Skelton, Viscount Bruce of Ampthill and 1st Earl of Ailesbury. He had been MP for the county during his father's time, and was to become its Lord Lieutenant and a Privy Councillor. His son Thomas, born in 1656, was even more closely connected to the court than his father, and held most of the same offices of state. He had grown up in close friendship with Charles I's children, and his subsequent loyalty to the Stuarts led to his eventual exile to Brussels, where in extreme old age he wrote his memoirs, frequently quoted in this history. He died in 1741.

Christiana, Countess of Devonshire

Lord Elgin's only sister was so named through having been born on Christmas Day in 1595. Her marriage to Sir William Cavendish, who became 2nd Earl of Devonshire in 1626, was short lived and blighted by serious financial troubles. He died within two years of marrying leaving two sons a daughter and massive debts to the care of his widow. After the countess died in January 1674, Lord Elgin's chaplain, Thomas Pomfret, wrote and published an account of her life, a delightful period piece of flowery prose and uninhibited flattery. (Pomfret, a minor poet of the period, was vicar of Luton but lived in Ampthill.) Although she spent most of her life after marriage on family estates in Derbyshire and elsewhere, she retired to her brother's house in Ampthill for three years from 1646 and kept up regular correspondence with her brother and nephew which has ensured the preservation of many local snippets of interest.

Thomas Pomfret, after a lengthy and effusive dedication of his work to Lord Devonshire, his subject's son, suggests his 'Narrative may yield some Profit and Delight to all but [except] such as come to it with Prejudice and Humour because it is a Ladies Life.' He recalls how the 'purity of her youth, the pregnancy of her wit and her freedom from passions' were widely admired, and puts the blame for her husband's inability to cope on his father's second marriage 'which too commonly brings disadvantage to the children of the first venture'. The young Sir William was soon in 'a very great debt . . . by an excess of gallantry . . . increased by the magnificence of his living both in town and country.'

His death at the age of 27 in 1628 left his widow with enormous debts and 30 lawsuits pending. 'But to that right which was on her side she added diligence and resolution and by these not only acquitted her self with the greatest bravery but prevailed in them all to the highest satisfaction' and with the moral support of her brother Elgin, cleared the estate of its mammoth debts. In daily life 'her gestures corresponded to her speech; no giddy head or proud eyelids, no laughing brow or perplexed countenance'. 'Prayers and pious readings were her first business . . . the remainders of the day were determined to her friends.'

In the civil war the family estates were sequestered. Her younger son, Colonel Charles Cavendish, was killed in action and her daughter Lady Rich (daughter-in-law to the Earl of Warwick) died and so, late in 1646 'being much depressed in mind with such a load of publick calamaties, she would try if privacy might give ease to any part of her sorrows. Retire therefore she did to her brother the Earl of Elgin's house at Ampthill, a place, if any in the world (next to her son's) that could compose her distracted thoughts.' For the next three years she lived at Ampthill (probably in Great Lodge) where she was deeply involved in political and church matters. 'The war had made loyalty poor, and sequestrations upon the priests of God had reduced the clergy to such lamentable wants that they had nothing left to cloath them but their own righteousness; nor any thing to feed on but a good conscience and their passive vertues . . . ' The countess used all her contacts and influence to support impoverished clergy and 'removed' fifty of the poor to her estate at Roehampton.

'During her abode at Ampthill she had continued correspondencies with such persons both in England and Scotland as she found would assist to the resettlement of the king and the recovery of the Church and State from those thraldoms under which they both groaned.' But 'though her actings were not thorowly discovered, yet so much suspected were they by the then usurped powers, that a troop of horse had been sent down to fetch her up from Ampthill (about the same time that the Countess of Carlisle was put into the Tower).' But she was forewarned by 'her goldsmith (a confident of the Rebells)' who had 'given a bribe to one of the then council of state, whose great licenstiousness and narrow fortunes rendred him greedy enough of money.'

'Escaping thus narrowly did not in the least abate but rather redouble her fortitude and reinforce her resolution not to give over till she had the fairest prospect in that critical time of General Monk's action. With him therefore she enters into a speedy and secret correspondency, and though he was one of a most retired and prudent wariness, yet so far he instructed her (which he did few besides) that he sent her by a considerable officer a private signal by which she might know his intentions . . .'[56]

The Nicolls Family
Francis Nicolls had been Squire of the Bath to Sir Edward Bruce and married his niece, Margaret, daughter of Sir George Bruce of Carnock, at Abbots Langley, Hertfordshire, in 1609, where the parish registers

record the baptism of five of their six children. He became Keeper of the Ampthill parks and lived with his family in the Great Lodge. Their eldest child was a daughter given her mother's maiden name as a first Christian name, Bruce (1611), who later married John Freschville, but died in 1629 at the age of 18. Another daughter, Elizabeth, was baptised 17th September 1616 but died a month later, and a son William, died in infancy. Three sons survived childhood, Edward (1614), Francis (1620) and Richard born at Great Lodge in the early part of 1625, several months after the death of his father the previous September.

In his will Francis Nicolls committed the care of his children to his widow and to Sir Thomas Bruce, his executors, adding 'for all my Children let none condeme me for their yeares are tender and I am not in possibility to live to see the fruits of their good disposition and carriage'. He asks that the 'Charitie towardes my brother William' be continued 'which my wife knowes what it is'. (Younger brother William, Doctor of Divinity and later (1644) Dean of Chester was known after the Restoration to Samuel Pepys as the Dean of Queens' College, Cambridge.) To his wife Margaret he left the park lease making her keeper in his place. He was buried in Ampthill church.

Richard Nicolls

The baptism of Richard is not recorded in the Ampthill registers, but following so soon after his father's death would have been conducted privately by Parson Reeve or Lord Bruce's chaplain at Great Lodge or in the chapel of Houghton House. His distinguished career is concisely summed up in the Latin of the memorial marking the tomb he shared with his parents. It tells how 'from the cradle he was intimate with the most illustrious James, duke of York' and the rest of the royal family. When the civil war began he was given the command of a troop of horse, while his brothers Francis and Edward led infantry regiments. All three brothers followed the Stuarts into exile on the continent where Edward and Francis died. Richard joined the duke of York's household and served with him during the civil wars (known as the Fronde) in France.

At the Restoration he returned to England and in 1663 was awarded a doctorate in civil law by Oxford University. The following year Charles II granted his brother James all the territory on the Atlantic coast of North America originally claimed by English explorers but then held by the Dutch, with the intention that it should be combined into a single province. A commission of four, led by Richard Nicolls (with a casting vote), was appointed to carry this out, and in June 1644, they set sail with a small task force of four frigates, 300 soldiers and some administrators. The chief settlement, New Amsterdam, despite the best efforts of its Dutch governor Peter Stuyvesant, was poorly and inefficiently administered and was defenceless. Its inhabitants, totally dejected and thoroughly demoralised, surrendered with little fuss to Richard Nicolls on 27th August 1664.

Colonel Nicolls renamed the settlement New York in honour of his friend and commander the duke of York, and for three years he ruled as its first English governor. He was remembered as a man of outstanding courtesy and consideration who gave the colony its first individual judicial code, establishing a court of assize modelled on English county quarter-sessions. One of his institutions surviving today is Trinity Church in Wall Street. Governor Nicolls retired after three years and returned to England and Ampthill where he is reputed to have built a house (long since demolished) where The Cloisters in Church Street is now.

In 1672 he was called to support James, then Lord High Admiral, at Sole Bay off Dunwich in Suffolk, where on 28th May, 'fighting bravely on the flagship against the Dutch, he was pierced by the stroke of a cannon ball and fell'. His body was brought back to Ampthill and buried in his parents' tomb in the parish church, the cannon ball, 'instrument of death and immortality', being built into his memorial.[57]

Richard Conquest
The Conquests, who gave their name to Houghton, had been established in the village since the 13th century. For several generations the head of the family had lived at Conquest Bury, a modest Tudor manor house

built into a fold of the north face of the greensand ridge just off the London Lane in Houghton Conquest where Bury Farm now stands. At the beginning of the 17th century this was the home of Sir Richard Conquest, his wife Dorothy (who had been one of the Hewetts of Ampthill – a strong recusant family) and over the years their 20 children. Sir Richard, who had been educated at Cambridge, played a major part in Bedfordshire affairs, was a magistrate, twice sheriff and a loyal Anglican. In 1603 he was knighted by James I who two years later stayed a couple of nights at the Bury and attended Houghton Church. Sir Richard died in 1617 and the following year king James knighted his elder son Edmund on appointing him keeper of the royal park at Houghton. Sir Edmund had married Elizabeth Sandys and like his father, was sheriff twice. [58]

Richard Conquest, born in 1597, was the eldest of their many children. In 1626 he married Elizabeth Thimelby of Irnham, Lincolnshire, a lady of the bedchamber to Queen Henrietta Maria and from a noted recusant family. By the time he succeeded his father in 1634 the estate was heavily in debt, due mainly to the large number of close relatives he had to support. On top of that were fines for recusancy (the Thimelbys remained loyal Catholics, and he had adopted his wife's faith).

Following the civil war, when he had been a colonel in the Royalist army, his estates were sequestered (taken into management by parliamentary officials to ensure payment of fines) in 1644 and 1650. By 1645 he had been in prison for debt and the following year was reported to the Bedfordshire Committee for reputedly threatening Goodwife Toach of Houghton Conquest 'with pistolles Cockt' in a desperate attempt to collect the rent owed him by her husband Thomas. And still the family dependants remained, by 1650 two brothers, two sisters, eight sons and five servants. [59]

In the complaints against Parson Reeve we hear of his friendship and frequent conversations with Richard Conquest and his wife which are given as evidence of Reeve's own recusancy. But a parson was expected to try to convert recusants 'using all good means he can devise.' [60]

Richard Conquest died in 1671 and was succeeded at Conquest Bury by his eldest son John. Many years later, the exiled Thomas Bruce, 2nd Earl of Ailesbury, writing his memoirs in Brussels noted 'As to Roman Catholicks there was not one in the County save Mr Conquest who lived obscurely . . .' Richard's grandson, Benedict, having no male issue, was the last to hold the manor. He moved to Irnham in Lincolnshire, the Thimelby family's seat. [61]

Benjamin Rhodes

Benjamin Rhodes, steward to the Earl of Elgin at Houghton House, was obviously a person of some standing locally and highly regarded by his employer to whom he claimed to be related. He had been responsible for the design and building of the Bruce Mausoleum at Maulden Church and died in 1657, a year after its completion, when Lord Elgin's chaplain, Peter Samwaies, gave a *Narration on the Exemplary Death . . .[of this] . . .Wise & Faithful steward*. From this we learn that he was 'competent' in Latin and French and 'very well skilled in Musick'. Serving with the Earl of Oxford in the Low Countries he was 'in the heat of skirmish suddenly struck with consideration of that execution that his bullets might make [and that] the killing of men is the worst of trades.' He then transferred to the service of Lady Oxford (who became Lord Elgin's second wife) and at the time of his death had been with the Elgins for 28 years.

The *Narration* speaks of him 'as a Christian . . . constant to his Principles . . . fixed upon the basic of the holy Scriptures, as interpreted by the Articles of the Church of England: in the communion of which . . . as he had received his Baptism, so he professed to lay down his life, intreating a neighbour that was in his chamber to signifie so much unto his acquaintance at Ampthill.' 'And this, Beloved,' continues the preacher, 'is a matter of great moment, to keep the union of the church in these times of Division and Schisme.' Mr Samwaies goes back to the theme on a number of occasions: 'Account your happiness to have been preserved in the union of this National Church in whose fellowship our dear brother departed professed himself to leave this world. I well know you may see much to be blamed in many of them that boast themselves to be sons of the Church of England. I wish all their spots were the spots of children . . .' (He must have been aware of the deceased's treatment of Hugh Reeve 17 years earlier, and was himself expelled by parliament from his vicarage at Cheshunt.) [62]

Elsewhere we hear 'how careful he [Rhodes] was to be present at the Domestick Chappel' in Houghton House, how deeply he involved himself in religious affairs and how 'our peaceable Brother abhorred and detested . . . casting out as Antichristian the Apostolical Government of the Church'. This was the principle that had moved him to petition parliament on 23rd February 1640/41, for the removal of the Ampthill's rector. The parish, he wrote then, 'hath for 40 years groaned under the burden of the Parson there, one Hugh Reeve, who . . . broacheth & maintaineth . . . ridiculous, blasphemous popish & Jesuitical opinions, conversing chiefly with papists & . . . attempting to pervert persons of quality from the true religion established.'

Benjamin Rhodes had married Anne Glover of Hertfordshire, 'a woman of excellent parts' who was sufficiently familiar with the French language to translate the whole Book of Psalms into French. Some of her poetry is printed as part of the *Narration* including 'An Elegy on my first child, still-born' (a daughter) in the form of an acrostic on RHODES which she presented to her husband on their wedding anniversary.

> *R eliques lye here inshrin'd of that chaste love*
> *H eavan & Providence united in us two*
> *O ur hopes perswade us she is plac't above.*
> *D eplore our losse too much we dare not doe.*
> *E re she posses't a grave she found her tomb*
> *S he was not, for God took her from the womb.*

Two sons survived to be educated at Westminster School.

Rhodes was 'an Husband . . . loving, tender, able and apt to teach and instruct his wife, free from bitterness and passion'. But on 24th July, 1657 he fell ill 'of a distemper' and increasingly feverish and delirious died on 3rd August 'about 11 a.m.' His wife Anne, 'diligently attending her Husband . . . sickened on 28th July and departed on 4th August a little after midnight, about two of the clock'. (It is not clear what the illness was, but Mr Samwaies praised God that he was recovered from it!) They were buried together in the north aisle of Maulden church 'at the entrance in to the lately erected Chappel for the Sepulchre of the Rt Hon Diana Countess of Oxford and Elgin on 4th August 1657 at the evening', although Rhodes' will had directed as an alternative the open churchyard on the north side 'to crosse the received superstition, as he thought, of the constant choice of the South Side.' [63]

The *Narration*, in the fashion of the day, dwells at length on the death bed scenes. 'Their carriage in the time of their sicknesse was very unlike and different one from the other, for whereas he was very startled in his assurance of the fruition of Christ, crying out every moment almost, I goe to my Christ, I goe to my God . . . She was grievously assaulted with the terrour of her sins, brought down to the gates of despair almost, so that I had much adoe by the best cordials that I could administer unto her out of the Gospel'. And while he 'continued almost to his last gasp in the sobriety of his mind, giving not only a good example, but holy advice to as many as came near him', for Anne Rhodes, doubtless remembering her husband's instruction, 'her sins were more odious unto her than death itself'.

Surprisingly for one who lived his life according to strict biblical precepts, death caught Benjamin Rhodes unawares and his will had to be drawn up after the distemper had taken hold. He was at first reluctant to sign and seal it on a Sunday, but when it was pointed out to him that his generous bequests to the poor of St John's (sic) and Maulden (£5 each) and Ampthill and Houghton Conquest (£2.10s each) were charitable acts, he agreed.

Edmund Wingate

Edmund Wingate, born and baptised at Flamborough, Yorkshire in 1596 was the second son of Roger Wingate of Sharpenhoe in Bedfordshire and his wife Jane. From Queen's College, Oxford, (BA 1614) he moved to Gray's Inn and the legal profession. Like so many young men of his generation he spent much time in France and was sufficiently fluent in the French language to be selected to teach English to Princess Henrietta Maria (later King Charles I's queen). In 1624 he published (in Paris) a French edition, hastily put together to anticipate plagiarism of his theories by a 'friend', of what in its English version was called *The Use of the Rule of Proportion*.

His biographer, Bertha Porter, notes thirteen of his 'numerous publications', seven of them mathematical, the rest on law. His first law work was a reference book compiled with magistrates in mind (he was a Bedfordshire JP), *A Table of Statutes now in force* (1641), followed the next year by an *Exact Abridgement of all the Statutes in force and use from the beginning of Magna Carta*. Later came *The Exact Constable with his Original and Power in the Office of Churchwardens* – offices he did not hold in Ampthill. His mathematical achievements were pioneering, with works on the construction and use of logarithm tables, including *Ludus Mathematicus* 'the description of a logarithmic instrument, of the nature of which it is difficult to form an idea without even a drawing of it', and *The Use of a Gauge-rod*. Small wonder that Edmund Wingate is credited with having invented (or 'popularised') the slide rule so recently made obsolete with the coming of calculators and computers.

In 1628 Wingate married (at Maulden) Elizabeth, daughter and heir of Richard Button of Wootton. They had five sons and two daughters. By this time the Honour of Ampthill was held by Queen Henrietta Maria, who in 1633/4 made her former English teacher her Warden, Bailiff and Coroner. A fine modern house in Church Street (now numbers 31 to 35A) with four acres of ground, formerly the home of Richard Hodgkis, steward of the Honour of Ampthill, was purchased and became Wingate's principal home for the rest of his life.

Within a few years Edmund Wingate had rejected his royal contacts and became a strong and zealous parliamentarian. He 'took the covenant' which was a commitment to a Presbyterian Church of England and became one of the commissioners for the ejection of ignorant and scandalous ministers (among whom he included in 1642 Hugh Reeve, Parson of Ampthill). In 1650 he 'took the engagement', the oath of loyalty to the Commonwealth 'without a King and House of Lords' required of all men of 18 and over. He became a friend of Oliver Cromwell, and also of the regicide John Okey (see below) whose letter 'For his Much Honored Friend Mr Wingate Esquire att his house in Ampthill' survives.

He became a Bedfordshire MP in 1654, but died at his house in Gray's Inn Lane, and was buried in Saint Andrew's Church, Holborn on 13th December, 1656.[64]

John Okey
Soon after the establishment of the Protectorate and the completion of the 1649 survey of crown lands, officers of the parliamentary army were able to acquire parts of the sequestered estates in lieu of back pay due to them. Thus, in 1650 the Ampthill, Millbrook and Brogborough manors were sold to John Okey, colonel of a regiment of dragoons in the New Model Army, and others of his regiment, for £2,041. 5s. 7½d. Colonel Okey, who had been proprietor of a ship's chandler's business near the Tower of London, was an Anabaptist (one of the earliest religious groups to separate from the Church of England) and spent much time when in Bedfordshire living at the lodge, or Round House, in Brogborough Park (burned down in 1993). He became a magistrate and officiated at many of the civil marriages which replaced the traditional church services during the Commonwealth, and his signature is still to be found in the registers.

Okey had been a commissioner at the trial of Charles I, whose death warrant he signed, and was one of the five who selected the time and place for the king's execution. He was strongly opposed to any attempt to give the Lord Protector absolute power, and in 1656 played a major part in preparing a petition 'The Humble and Serious Testimony of many hundreds of godly well-affected people in Bedfordshire . . .' opposed to the proposal to make Cromwell king.

In 1656 he was admonished by the council on suspicion of intrigue and the following year, with other republicans, spent a brief period in the Tower of London under suspicion for plotting. But in 1658 he sat as member for Bedfordshire in Richard Cromwell's parliament, and the following year was sent to Gloucester as military commander of the area. In 1660, just before the Restoration, Okey fled to the continent and settled for a time at Hanau in Hesse-Nassau, but was brought back to England to face trial for his part in the execution of Charles I through the duplicity of Sir George Downing, ambassador at the Hague under the Protectorate. (Okey had made Downing – after whom the famous London street was named – chaplain of his dragoon regiment in the early days of the civil war, and subsequently took him under his wing.) John Okey was tried as a regicide (one responsible for Charles I's execution), sentenced to death, and on 19th April 1662 he was hung at Tyburn. After a quarter of an hour on the gibbet he was cut down and quartered, his dismembered parts being taken to Newgate to be boiled!

Colonel John Okey
from a rare drawing.
(See note 65.).

In prayer before his execution he had asked that Charles II might 'live in the sight of God and be a nursing father to his people and a friend of religion'. On the king's orders he was buried in the chapel of Saint Peter ad Vincula in the Tower of London. [65]

8

Parson Reeve

'Christmas day, the weather being somewhat cold, he tould his parishioners
that he had entended to have given them a sermon, but . . . he would have
them know that he had a care as well of their bodies as their soules,
therefore would defere it till another occasion,
and divers other such like stuffe . . . '
Article 41 of Benjamin Rhodes' petition to parliament 23ʳᵈ February, 1640/1

It is paradoxical that if Hugh Reeve's opponents had not petitioned
parliament we should know considerably less about him, them and Ampthill
than we do now. But in the 41 Articles and two Petitions drawn up to
bring about his expulsion (printed in Appendix A), we can follow his
teaching, hear echoes from his sermons, and see him ministering to the
pastoral needs of his flock – as he had done for 40 years during which,
Benjamin Rhodes would have it, the people of Ampthill had 'groaned
under the burden of the Parson'.

Biographical
It has not been possible to establish firmly the details of Hugh Reeve's
birth (note 66 elaborates) but it must have been in the 1560s. He could
not have been ordained priest until he was 24, and would have served a
curacy or two before coming to Ampthill in 1600, when he would have
been in his 30s. Article 20 says he had been ordained by Toby Matthew
when Bishop of Durham, which was between 1595 and 1606. The
Durham ordination registers for this period have been lost, and in his
diary the bishop limits himself to inclusive phrases such as 'ordained
many curates', so a precise date cannot be fixed. At the time of
ordination Article 20 says Reeve was in the Bishop of Lincoln's service,
perhaps as domestic chaplain – 'butler' according to his detractors.

(The puritans liked to belittle a priest's status and educational qualification – as they saw it - by placing him in a humble domestic background). It is possible he was prepared for ordination under some sort of sizarship, receiving instruction in return for undertaking chores to earn his keep. In the introduction to his petition to parliament Benjamin Rhodes complained that Reeve 'understands scarce a word of Latin', which would have been a disadvantage to a papist. But this is the judgement of a detractor who, according to his funeral *Narration* (Chapter 7), was obviously proud of his own 'competence' in the language. Although by the 1630s Hugh Reeve wore the Cambridge MA hood when he read prayers, he does not appear among the regular university alumni, and a 1603 return confirms that he was not a graduate. But if what Article 40 says is true, he was awarded what was called a Mandate degree, conferred on royal instructions by James I.[66]

Hugh Reeve was presented to Living of Ampthill (then in the diocese of Lincoln) by Elizabeth I on 3rd October 1600, following the departure of Alexander Stockwell (listed as a recusant in 1599) whose resignation deed he had witnessed at Buckden, the Bishop of Lincoln's palace in Huntingdonshire. The institution, by the Bishop of Lincoln (presumably in his chapel at Buckden) took place on 13th November following, when a mandate was issued for Reeve's induction at Ampthill by the Archdeacon of Bedford. Article 20 reports Alexander Stockwell 'hath often reported' that Hugh Reeve had 'obtained the parsonage of Ampthill ... by indirect meanes', whatever that meant. But Stockwell's resignation document, read before the Public Notary at Buckden, states that he had 'true, just and legitimate reasons' for resigning – he had been rector for 34 years, which would be a more than adequate reason.[67]

Family
Queen Elizabeth was definitely not in favour of married clergy, and when Hugh Reeve married Ann (who died in 1614) he would have needed the approval of his bishop – and two magistrates. By the time of their arrival in Ampthill they had at least five children, William, John, Amy, Ann and a daughter Revell (perhaps her mother's maiden name). John,

who received £10 in his father's will 'if he be living at the time of my deathe', is a bit of a mystery as a second son also called John was born at Ampthill in 1603 and died there five years later. Other children born at Ampthill were Thomas (1604), Elizabeth (1606) and Richard (1607-1611). Neither Thomas nor Elizabeth are mentioned in their father's will (1646 – Appendix B) and must be presumed to have died. A grandson Richard Reeve, who received £25, must have been William's son. Other grandchildren mentioned were John and Robert Sanders (baptised at Ampthill in 1639 and 1640 respectively) the sons of Ann who had married John Sanders, gentleman, in 1638. Revell Reeve remained unmarried and was living with her father at the time of his death. She died at Ampthill in 1656.[68]

Amy Reeve married twice. Her first husband was John Drommond, described as 'clerk' (clergyman) in the register recording the baptism of their daughter Mary in 1631 and the baptism and burial of their son John in 1633. When their son David was baptised (and buried) in 1635 he is referred to as 'gent.'. Article 27 describes John Drommond as 'an excommunicated parson . . . a turbulent and contentious person', while Article 34 notes that he had served as proctor when Hugh Reeve held court as the bishop's surrogate. The full story behind his change of status from 'clerk' to 'gent' has not come to light. Drommond died in 1636, and three years later Amy married Edmund Ruffhead, gentleman, who had property in Church Square (site of Brandreth House). Their son Edmund, born in 1640, did not survive the year. Edmund senior was churchwarden in 1640 and in 1646 Hugh Reeve's executor.

Ecclesiastical Duties

In about 1610 the Bishop of Lincoln made Hugh Reeve responsible for collecting together the annual register transcripts of christenings, marriages and burials for the whole of the archdeaconry and delivering them to the bishop's office at Buckden. By 1637 the local puritan clergy had withdrawn their co-operation so he petitioned Archbishop Laud to direct 'that he may receive the said certificates as formerly'. For more than 30 years as the bishop's surrogate he was responsible for holding the church courts and dealing with complaints according to canon law – which made it very difficult for anyone to complain about the rector. Article 34 suggests rough and ready organisation. He 'kept a Court without a Register, appointed a woman to be his apparitor' (court messenger – the puritans placed great emphasis on Saint Paul's instructions on the place of women in the church) and that he 'had no proctor but one Dromond his sonne in lawe an excommunicate person.' Furthermore, his judgements were compassionate rather than examples of Divine Wrath and Vengeance, for he 'gave sentence that one Susan Dearman should aske one Tymothy Bayly forgivenesse and did there also acquit one Mrs Williams of a crime of fornication commited with one Thoroughgood a minister.' As for religious offences, 'he hath preached in the pulpit . . . that he will spend all he hath to a groate to defend himself . . . and threatneth all persons which dislike his doctrine with suits of law, and hath sued divers of them . . . he being there a surrogate and having very great party amongst them to bring Grists to their mills.'[69]

Ampthill church from the north in 1817, the churchyard's northern boundary hedge being clearly seen. The Parsonage stood in the plot where three trees are growing. The building on the left is the Town House where the Reeves lived after the Parsonage had been burnt down.

The Parsonage

In 1708 it was noted that Ampthill's 'Parsonage House, according to the best accounts from the oldest people in the parish, was burnt down (tho' before their memories) & never since rebuilt. And stood at the lower end of a Pightle [small enclosed plot] adjoyning to the north side of the Churchyard.' No description of the house survives, but it would have been similar to Millbrook's, which in 1708 was timber framed 'and covered with tiles & contains four bays wherein are a parlour & study floored with board an hall, kitchen, dairy, buttery & a little spare roome floored with brick & four upper rooms floored with boards two whereof are cieled.' In addition there would have been outbuildings as at Steppingley: 'a barne of two bayes clay walls and clay floores & thatched with a lean too at the end . . . with a small hogstye & stable clay-walls & thatched, a pightle, yard & garden adjoyning.' It was a big enough house to accommodate the Reeve family and a servant or two, and for entertaining visiting church dignitaries, such visits being recorded in the parish register by the rector.

On 27th September, 1612, the Bishop of Lincoln, William Chaderton, preached at Ampthill 'and lodged 2 nights in Mr Reevs house then paster of Ampthill.' The bishop was back the following January for three nights while sitting on a commission of charitable uses (a sub- committee of the Privy Council) and was here again for a night in August 1613. George Abbott, whose nephew Robert Abbott lived at Steppingley Park, 'lodged 3 nights in the house of the said Mr Reeve,' when Bishop of London. Sir Nathaniel Brent, Archbishop Laud's Vicar General, stayed for three nights during the 1634 visitation, and the following August Bishop John Williams stopped for two nights on the occasion of the preaching of the controversial *Sunday no Sabbath* and *Priest's Duty and Dignity* sermons. Soon after this the parsonage house burnt down.

It is unrealistic not to connect the burning down of the parsonage with the harrying and bullying Hugh Reeve was receiving from some of his parishioners in their efforts to have him removed from office, and the explanation given in 1708 from 'the best accounts from the oldest people' that its burning down was 'before their memories', is quite unconvincing. The incident must have taken place shortly before 1640, and a ten-year-old from that time would be 68 in 1708. An enquiry into rights on the warren in 1607 questioned seven witnesses whose average age was 65, so there should have been no difficulty a hundred years later, in finding enough people to say exactly what had happened to the parsonage little over 50 years before, and who had been responsible. Fires live long in the folk memory, and the tactful gloss that the explanation was from the 'best accounts' makes it clear that there were other accounts, and that more *could* have been recorded about this sinister incident.

The Town House

It was fortunate that Hugh Reeve and his unmarried daughter Revell were able to move into a Town House adjoining the churchyard soon after the destruction of the parsonage. It did not belong to the church but for nearly two hundred years had been administered by the Feoffees to house the poor and needy. The accommodation rented by the Reeves would have included the property now known as number 1, and perhaps a bit more (there was extensive remodelling in the 19th century). Their possessions were very few, and a great deal must have been lost in the fire or disposed of subsequently. In his will, made on 20th January, 1645/6, (Appendix B) Parson Reeve leaves his son William the best bedstead, with its feather mattress, bolster, pillow, pillowcase and three blankets. The bed had green curtains and valance and there was a green rug. Revell inherited a feather bed, a blanket, coverlet, white rug, a brass pot, a table and three stools 'and all the furniture in the chamber wherein I now lye'. As an afterthought further on in the will she receives a bedstead, curtains and valance, a pair of holland sheets, a pillowcase and three pieces of pewter – perhaps the contents of her own room. William also has his father's desk. The long gown, which was part of his formal clothing, (see Appendix C) went to make clothes for his grandchildren, while his two short gowns were given to daughter and daughter-in-law. Daughter Amy received a canopy – part of the bed hangings. There is no mention of books. There wouldn't have been many - perhaps they had been destroyed in the fire.

Teaching

The complaint made about Anglican clergy not preaching enough was a common one and led to the puritans setting up weekly 'lectures' in the main towns. At Ampthill lectures were given in the church by 'divers ministers' but presumably without the rector's approval. Article 36 tells how after Parson Reeve had read prayers he 'went out of the Church when any of these Ministers went up into the pulpit . . . in a very arrogant & presumptuous manner . . .' Article 13 reports how Thomas Blyeth used to go to Hawnes to hear the preacher, and when asked why said it was 'to increase his knowledge', to which the parson responded, 'God hath given thee knowledge and learning, and the Divell hath gott within thee and leads thee to Hawnes . . .' And to James Woodward he is reported to have said that 'it was better for him to steal one of his master's sheep than to go out of his own parish to hear a sermon . . .' (Article 14).

It has to be remembered that the complaints were compiled by people determined to show Parson Reeve in the worst possible light as part of their attempts to have him removed from office, and it is surprising that the accounts of conversations and incidents, some of which had taken place over twenty years before (see Chapter 6), were not more garbled than they obviously are.

The Canons ordered a sermon every Sunday with catechising in the afternoon, and a return of 1603 notes that Parson Reeve 'catechiseth' and that his 'behaviour' was 'good'. But according to his detractors, he only preached six or seven times a year 'for the most part in the Holy time of Lent as hee calleth it' (Article 30). Prayer, he is quoted as saying, 'is to be preferred before preaching, for by it many excellent and wonderful things have been done . . . [while] preaching is but a hand in a post pointing out the way to a town, but never brings [it] thither . . . it is not the service of God, I say againe it is not the service of God.' (Article 2). (Note the repetition for emphasis, a characteristic of some preachers and politicians to this day, and obviously typical of Hugh Reeve as it occurs again in Article 33).

Elsewhere we find aspects of the rector's orthodox Prayer Book teaching (1549 rather than 1552) with some over-emphasis perhaps where puritans were looking for a papist: the soul's relationship to God (Article 5), Transubstantiation and the Immaculate Conception (Article 1), the Virgin Mary (Article 10), repentance (Article 8), priestly authority (Articles 17 and 19), the authority of the Church (Article 7), and Patron Saints (Article 3).

In a Lent sermon the Rector reminded his congregation 'that the due observance of all fasting and Embering days . . . is a service that God requires at our hands in payne of damnation contrary to the proviso of 5 Eliz 5.' [70] Later, in reference to infant baptism, 'saith he, no man shall be damned for ignorance, for ignorance shall condemne no one.' (Article 6). 'And in his sermons on Easter Day remarked that it was the highest Sunday of the year [and] because [of that] the next following is called Low Sunday,' (Article 41) which remains the accepted explanation for the day's unusual name.

On Christmas Day 1640 (Article 18) he preached 'that God took upon him the shape of man and was Adam's companion in paradise . . . that God was the first and the Virgin Mary the second cause of our redemption, that Adam was made of the virgin earth and our Saviour was born of the Virgin Mary'. 'And another time upon a Christmas Day the weather being somewhat cold [churches were unheated] he told his parishioners that he had intended giving them a sermon, but the weather was very cold, and he would have them know that he had a care as well for their bodies as their souls therefore would defer it till another occasion . . .' (Article 41) . . . 'and divers other such stuff, all which here to relate . . . would seeme both tedious and impertinent (last word crossed out and in another hand 'troublesome' substituted).

Personal Faith
We hear of his personal devotion from Article 32, of 'his usuall gestures when he cometh into the Church as crossing himself, cringing and ducking [genuflecting] and kneeling at the rayles before the Altar (as he calleth

it).' When, probably in his late 60s, he was seriously ill and thought likely to die, he sent for a sympathetic priest to hear his confession (Article 24). During this illness he was off duty for six weeks, his daughter Amy's husband, John Drommond, acting as locum (Article 27). But his critics saw this as malingering and evidence of a defection to Rome. After a while 'Thomas Cookson Doctor of Divinity a grave minister' rector of Millbrook, visited. He was reported to have had the backing of the bishop in an attempt to persuade the invalid 'to conforme himself and to come to church againe . . . lest that he should loose his living'. (Wasn't that the critics' aim?) The fact that the parson resumed his duties shortly after suggests a better state of health rather than fear of dismissal.

Much of Dr Cookson's involvement as reported here must be speculation. Neighbourly and fraternal concern would be expected, but not collusion with the puritan camp. The doctor, who was also rector of Marston, was thrown out of his parishes in 1643 for 'preaching subjection and refusing the Covenant' (see page 84). He took himself off to Oxford to study physic, and is last heard of as a Royalist prisoner following the fall of Sherborne Castle.[71]

It is not clear how many Ampthill people supported the complaints against the parson. Most of the parishioners who did not throw themselves whole-heartedly into the puritan movement (or owe their employment to Benjamin Rhodes's stewardship of the Bruce estate) would keep their heads down and carry on as usual, for so long as they were able. Article 39 talks of 'a strong faction of papists' in the area, but only three families are known, the Watsons of Little Park and Beckerings Park, the Hewetts of the Grange and the Conquests. Hugh Reeve's friendship and ministry to these, comes in for a great deal of criticism. We hear how (Article 22) 'many a night and other times they have walked three or four hours together during which time the said Hugh Reeve did what he could to persuade Richard Conquest to be a papist' – surely unnecessary when he'd married one. (How could observers at a distance know what was discussed?) And how one fasting day (Article 23) 'the said Rich

Conquest's wife excused how cheare [cheer – food for guests] being fish' Reeve 'told them both he loved fish very well and was very a papist as either of them', an incident that must have been reported by a gossiping servant. Canon 66 specifically orders 'Ministers to confer with Recusants'.

There are complaints (Article 29) that the Watson children of Little Park and Thomas Burge's children had been baptised privately 'in the popish manner' (as the Prayer Book permitted) in their own homes with 'none present . . . but only such as have always absented themselves from Church and professed themselves to be popish recusants.' Again, it is reported (Article 28) that Parson Reeve had buried 'divers persons in the chancel, church and churchyard . . . who in their lifetimes professed themselves to be papists . . .' and that he wrote 'earnestly' to the Vicar of Westoning endorsing the burial there of an excommunicate papist. (An excommunicate could not be buried in a churchyard, but had to be put in a field or on waste land. As a rule papists were not excommunicated.)

Benjamin Rhodes's petition and charge against Hugh Reeve was presented to parliament on 23rd February 1640/41. Papers with the petition say that he was found guilty but dealt with 'leniently', deprived of the living, ordered to recant and awarded a 'small' annuity of £10 a year out of the Living, but as it was not worth £30 a year 'a Noble person of the parish [Benjamin Rhodes's employer] freely offered to discharge it himself.' (In 1603 the value of the Living had been £10.6s.8d.) A draft warrant for the arrest of Hugh Reeve was not executed, although many other clergy in a similar situation later ended up in prison, among them Timothy Archer, rector of Meppershall (see Chapter 2). But Parson Reeve stood firm and the following year Edmund Wingate petitioned that he was still in the Town House, although 'requested on three separate occasions by divers of the Inhabitants' to give up the house refused to do so, so that John Howe, the intruded minister, was forced to rent a less convenient one for £7 a year. Obviously there had been a confrontation, perhaps before Wingate as a Commissioner for the Ejection of Ignorant and Scandalous Ministers, when an attempt to extract a recantation had been made, but 'in making his recantation [Reeve] did rather seem to maintain than recant his erroneous tenets, and did affirm to this deponent that he would still maintain two of those tenets which he then recanted and that he is still Parson of Ampthill . . .'

Duty Done

We can only guess at the pressures and bullying and intimidation and ill-treatment used to try to persuade him to change his beliefs and practices before the appeal to the House of Lords. But Parson Reeve battled on until when about 80 years old, time did what his opponents had failed to do and brought him low. On 27th January, 1645/6, with friends and family crowded into his little room in the Town House adjoining the churchyard, he dictated his will (Appendix B). The penitential introductory testament and patriotic dating in the 'Raiyne of our Soveruiyne Lord King Charles of England Scotland Fraunce and Ireland' were typical of his style as revealed in his opponents' complaints, and afterthought interlinings may be excused in old age.

His possessions (as bequeathed to his surviving children) were limited by the restricted accommodation to necessities, but he was able to bequeath a handsome sum of money totalling £161.13s.8d. The will was signed in the presence of Richard Wheeler and William Underwood, tailor, but the 'true and lawful Parson' lived on for ten months, his son in law Edmund Ruffhead being granted probate on 21st November, 1646.

And so into History

The survival of the petition to parliament calling for Hugh Reeve's removal from his post has led to his arbitrary and unjust treatment by commentators, who have based their judgements solely on the opinions of his detractors. Conversely, their evidence shows him to have been a conscientious parish priest and a servant to the wider church (albeit in a different tradition) for almost half a century, who stuck firmly to his beliefs and principles despite increasing years and infirmity. Parson Reeve ranks high in the list of Ampthill worthies!

Excursus

Religious Background
(*Contributed*)

The English Reformation came about because King Henry VIII was desperate for a male heir, for he feared that the country would lapse into civil war again if he left only a daughter. To the end of his days his own view of religion remained very much that of the Catholic faith in which he had been brought up, what today we would call Roman Catholicism. However, because the current Pope (then under the influence of England's enemies) refused to annul Henry's marriage to Katherine of Aragon (widow of his dead brother) which would have allowed him to marry the pregnant Anne Boleyn, Henry broke with the Papacy. As a result of this break, he allowed certain Protestant policies to be implemented – a liturgy in English and an English translation of the Bible. It is unlikely that he himself had much sympathy with the new Protestant doctrines gaining force on the continent, but many of his most influential courtiers were strongly Protestant, and under his infant son, Edward VI, they gained control of the government.

At the same time the reformers on the continent, in particular Luther in Germany and later Calvin in Geneva, had an increasing influence on certain of the English middle class. The first to be affected were the London and the east coast merchants because they or their agents travelled abroad and met foreign Protestants and were excited by the new teachings, and merchants were in a position to smuggle through the ports the books of the Reformers. Bedfordshire was an area (being not much more than 50 miles from the capital) where many London merchants invested their profits in the best of all securities, land, and so the Bedfordshire country gentry tended to keep their links with the City of London and to favour the new teachings. Cambridge University was one where many of the young dons had strong Protestant sympathies and these spread to their students, and you find that many of the Bedfordshire clergy were Cambridge graduates. Both of these classes influenced those they met, especially the more literate farmers and tradesmen, and in time Bedfordshire was one of the counties most strongly in favour of the new teachings.

Under Edward VI's guardians the country moved to an extreme Protestant position, but he was soon succeeded by his Roman Catholic elder sister. Queen Mary quickly put the country once more under the jurisdiction of the Pope at Rome, but her policy of burning convinced Protestants alienated many ordinary people, and in time *Foxe's Book of Martyrs* (of which there should have been a copy in every church) taught the English laity to fear the power of the Pope. The fact that the Geneva of Calvin was perhaps the most hospitable of the refuges that received the English reformers escaping abroad during Mary's reign, meant that on her death the Protestant clergy returning had been much influenced by Calvinism. Calvin's teaching had a strong emphasis on Predestination, and brought about a parish system under which the local church and minister and elders had total control over all who lived within its bounds. Church synods and assemblies had replaced the bishops and archbishops of pre-Reformation Europe, who were still retained in the English church. Thus many English Protestants, influenced by Calvin, wanted a church run along Genevan (and later Scottish) lines, where bishops had been abolished and replaced by a synodical system. These men comprised the puritan party which was the main force against the King in the English Civil War.

A large part of the English population still wished for the religious practices of their youth, the ritual, processions, saints' day observances, and the church ales and May dancing. A puritan parson, as in Northill, could in twenty years get rid of all these, whatever the ordinary people thought or wanted. On the other hand many of the clergy had little liking for extreme Protestant views, and kept as much as they could of pre-Reformation attitudes to God and the church.

Both parties had quite legitimate backing for their views, as the church settlement of the reign of Queen Elizabeth contained material that could support both sides. The extreme Calvinists could quote the 39 Articles, which taught much of what they believed. The old fashioned catholic party looked at the rubrics, which allowed them certain vestments and proper traditional ways of holding services. Thus later on Reeve, accused of consorting too much with recusants (the name for those remaining faithful to the Catholicism in communion with the Pope) could point to the instruction in the Church of England canon 66 that an incumbent should 'confer with Recusants [and] labour diligently with them from time to time, thereby to reclaim them from their errors . . . using all good means he can devise'. However, the extreme Protestants could suggest that Reeve found the recusants more sympathetic to his old-fashioned views than were the extreme puritans among his parishioners.

Appendix A

Parliament Petitioned

The notes for this Appendix are on page 112.

On 23rd *February, 1640/1, Benjamin Rhodes petitioned parliament for the removal of Hugh Reeve from the Rectory of Ampthill accompanying the petition with 41 "Articles" of complaint.*

The petition of Benjamin Rhodes
To the Right Honourable the Lords Spirituall & Temporall
assembled in his Majesty's High Court of Parliament
The humble petition of Benjamin Rhodes of Ampthill in the Countie of Bedford Gent on the behalfe of himselfe & other the Parishoners there. Most humbly sheweth, that whereas that Parish hath for Fortie yeares together, groaned under the burthen of the Parson there, one Hugh Reeve Clarke, who preacheth not above 6 or 7 times in the yeare and that for the most part in the holy time of Lent (as he calleth it) And professeth himselfe an enemy to preaching; understands scarce a word of Latin; broacheth & maintaineth both in his Sermons and discourse ridiculous, blasphemous, popish & Jesuitical opinions, Conversing chiefly with Papists and also perverting or (at least) attempting to pervert persons of quality from the true Religion established, to the Romish Religion; doth what he can to stirr up dissention amongst his neighbours; hath beene (and is still likely to continue) very troublesome amongst his said neighbours haveing comenced & prosecuted divers causelesse suits against them. All which will more plainly appeare upon the proofe of 41 Articles hereunto annexed.

And whereas heretofore the Parishoners there did make complaint of theise or the like grievances to Episcopall authority, but could then obtain noe redresse therein, by reason hee from time to time (by his insinuation) gained the favour of the Archbishops & Bishops for the time being, & for that of late daies, the said Parishoners had not incouragement at all to proceed that way (by reason of the times) especially hee having now by the space of 30 yeares together beene from time to time, Surrogate to the Chancellors and Comissaries of the Diocese.

Your Petitioner in all humble manner doth most humbly beseech your Lordships to Commiserate the said Parishoners condition, by a due and strict examination of the proofes of the said Articles, And to be a meanes that they for the time to come may bee eased of so intollerable a burthen; And that your Lordships would be pleased to provide that noe such ignorant, Popish & unworthie person may be hereafter admitted into the Ministrie as in your wisdomes shall be thought meet, And according to his bounden duty he & they shall daily pray.   Ben: Rhodes.

Certaine Articles against Hugh Reeve Clerke, Parson of Ampthill in the County of Bedd: whereby (amongst other things) it doth plainly appeare that hee is in hart a popish Recusant.

1.   First hee maintaineth that the bread & wine delivered in the Sacrament after Concecration is turned into the very body and blood of Christ by way of transubstantiation, comparing that as no man can tell how the Virgin Mary could conceive with child by the holy ghost over-shaddowing her noe more can any man tell how the Bread & Wine are turned into flesh and blood.

2.   Item that prayer is to bee preferred before preaching, for by it many excellent and wonderfull things have been done but by preaching neither evill hath beene removed from any man nor good procured to any one, as that preaching is but as a hand in a post pointing out the way to a towne, but never brings thether, for it is not the service of God, I say againe it is not the service of God.

3.   Item hee preached at Millbrooke feast being the next Sunday after Michaelmasse day and taught there that every feast and Church was dedicated unto one St. or another, so for example this feast is dedicated unto St Michaell and alwayes kept on the Sunday next following the Saints

day, and likewise that every Kingdome is dedicated unto one St or another as England to St George St Davy for Wales, St Denis for France, & St Patrick for Ireland, and that all these Sts sitt in heaven making intercession for the preservation and protection of the sayd kingdomes.

4. Item the breach of the second table is greater than the breach of the first.[1]

5. Item that God did give unto man a Soule out of his owne essence and being.

6. Item that if a Child be Baptised and live the course of nature 60 or 80 yeares, & dy before he commit actuall sin he shall be saved, for saith hee, no man shall bee damned for ignorance, for ignorance shall condeme none.

7. Item that whatsoever the Church commandeth, wee must obey without asking why soe, for saith hee the Church cannot erre.

8. Item that a man may bee in the state of true saving grace and salvation and yet finally totally and wholy fall away, and be dammed, and rise againe by repentance and be in state of grace and salvation.

9. Item that the outward act of Baptisme with the words of the institution thereof pronounced by the meanest or silliest priest is of itselfe powerfull and sufficient to conferre grace upon the child that is Baptised and instate him into salvation.

10. Item that the Virgin Mary was without all sinne originall, and actuall, for saith hee, for originall sinne she was sanctified in her mothers wombe as Jeremiah and John Baptist were, and for her actuall sinne wee have noe text of Scripture to proove that ever she commited any.

11. Item upon his text taken out of Romans 13 verse 13 walke honesty &c he spake with harte greefe that the greatest part lived in drunkenese

tipling whoreing and sermon hunting, which were complayned of by the Apostle out of the 3 Phil 18 & 19 verses whose end is damnation.[2]

12.   Item hee saith it is a greater sinne for a man to goe from his owne parish Church on the Saboth day than to sit in an Alehouse drinking & playing at Cards or dice on the Saboth day.

13.   Item he having conferense with Thomas Blyeth,[3] why saith hee do you goe Sermons, who answered to increase his knowledg; I knowe saith hee that God hath given thee knowledg and learning and the Divell hath gott within thee and leads thee to Hawnes to heare sermons, but if thou dost use this thou wilt prove an arrant knave or a beggar, for there is none that doth goe, but prooves beggars or knaves, die dumb or mad.

14.   Item hee sayd to James Woodward it was better for him to steale one of his Masters sheepe than to goe out of his owne parish to hear a sermon.

15.   Item the breach of a Holy day is as great a Sinne as the breach of the Saboth day, and that an holy day happening on the Sabboth maketh the Sabbath the higher day.

16.   Item that noe man can bee assured of his salvation in this life yea St Paul himselfe was not asured thereof.

17.   Item that hee hath often delivered in his sermons that by the heate of hellfire precyous scenes and Crimenalls are engendred in the bowells of the earth and that a priest is in dignity above the king especially in the Administration of the Sacrament because sayth hee, hee that giveth is more worthy than he that receives and he that standeth is more worthy than he that kneeles.

18.   Item that he the sayd Hugh Reeve upon Christmas Day 1640 delivered in his sermon that God took upon him the shape of a man and was Adams Companion in parradise: that the Church that is sayth he the

priest and the gospell hath power to bind Kings in Chaines, and nobles with linkes of Iron that God was the first and the Virgin Mary the second cause of our redemption, that Adam was made of Virgin earth and our Saviour was borne of the Virgin Mary.[4]

19. Item that the sayd Hugh Reeve accounts himselfe the best man in the parish, and hath tould a Noble Earle[5] who liveth there to his face that when hee delivers him the Sacrament he is a better man than hee.

20. Item that he the said Hugh Reeve; being at first only a Butler in the then Bishop of Lincolnes house was made Minister as he saith, by Toby Mathew[6] then Bishop of Duresme his Lord & master being as it seemes ashamed to doe it in the face of his Bishoppricke at or about that time and obtaine the parsonage of Ampthill aforesayd by indirect meanes as Alexander Stockwell the then Incombent hath often reported.

21. Item that the inhabitants of Ampthill aforesaid have heretofore made complaint of these or the like greivances to Episcopall authority but could never obtaine any redresse therein by reason he the sayd Hugh Reeve from tyme to tyme by his infirmation gained the favour of the Arch-bishops & Bishops for the tyme being & hath now by the space of thirty yeares togeather from tyme to tyme byn Surrogate to the Chancellor & Comissiaries of this Diocese or part thereof, whereby hee hath bene the better enabled to mayntayne popish tenetts without contradiction to trouble his neighbors and shelter the papists.[7]

22. Item that he the sayd Hugh Reeve was the first that ever proved Richard Conquest[8] of Houghton Conquest in the sayd County of Bedd: Esquire to bee a papist, and that many nights & other tymes they have walked 3 or 4 houres togeather during wych tyme the said Hugh Reeve did what he could to perswade Richard Conquest to be a papist.

23. Item that at another tyme when the sayd Richard Conquest had altered his religion & turned papist the sayd Hugh Reeve coming to the sayd Mr Conquests house upon a fasting day, the sayd Richard Conquests

wife excused how cheare being fish, he the sayd Hugh Reeve tould them
both that he loved fish very well and was as very a papist as either of
them.

24.　Item one Mr East a proctor now deceased dwelling at Weston in
Bucking: a reputed papist tould his daughter now the wife of Mr James a
minister in Kent upon his death bedd that he had taken that sicknesse
whereof he shortly after died by riding in the night to cary a popish preist
to take the Confession of the said Hugh Reeve, then sicke & in danger of
death.

25.　Item that hee the sayd Hugh Reeve being so confessed by a popish
preist & reconsiled to the Church of Rome after his recovery from his
sicknesse for 6 weekes togeather or thereabouts did absent himselfe from
Church and in stead of repayring thither hee did for the most part spend
the whole Sunday from morning till night in a house of the parish of Ampthill
aforesayd where the wife and children were and still are strong recusants.

26.　Item that Thomas Cookson[9] Doctor of Divinity a grave minister of
the next parish having notice thereof and the sayd Hugh Reeve confessing
unto him that he had changed his religion and beene Confessed as aforesayd
the sayd Doctor Cookson did Admonish the sayd Hugh Reeve to conforme
himselfe and to come to Church againe to execute his function, which hee
refusing to doe, and continuing still in his popish course of life the sayd
Doctor Cookson made complaint thereof to the now Bpp of Lincolne
after which complaint the sayd Hugh Reeve came to Church againe: But
before he did it he the sayd Hugh Reeve went to the sayd Richard Conquest
and tould him hee could not avoyd going to Church least that hee should
loose his living.

27.　Item that dureing the tyme of his sicknesse and this his absence
from Church , he the sayd Hugh Reeve appointed prayers to be read in his
Church by an excommunicated parson named John Drommond[10] his son
in law a turbulent and contentious person.
28.　Item that he the sayd Hugh Reeve hath buried divers persons in the

Channsoll Church and Churchyard of Ampthill aforesayd who within there life tymes professed themselves to bee papists and one amongst the rest wch lived and dyed a convicted recusant, and that hee the sayd Hugh Reeve did earnestly write unto the minister of Wesening in the sayd County of Bedf: for the burying of a papist in his Church or Churchyard that dyed there excommunicated, and afirmed by his letter that he might lawfully doe it.

29.   Item that at Mr Watsons House and at the House of Thomas Burges[11] in the parish of Ampthill aforesaid where papists doe inhabitt diverse Children have bene Christned by the sayd Hugh Reeve privately after the popish manner as hath bene vehemently suspected by reason none were suffered to be present thereat but only such as have allwayes absented themselves from Church and professed themselves to be popish recusants.

30.   Item that hee the sayd Hugh Reeve being a preaching minister or rather a preist as hee tearmeth himselfe should according to the Cannon preach at least once every Sunday and Catechise in the afternoones hee preacheth not above six or seaven tymes in a yeare and for the most part in the holy time of Lent (as hee calleth it) and then ordinarily such doctrines as is herein expressed and that if any of his parish goe to any other Church he causeth them to be troubled in the Eclesisticall courts for it.

31.   Item that Revill Reeve[12] one of his daughters is a papist and hath divrs times for sundry monethes togeather remayned in his house and all that tyme she hath not come to Church.

32.   Item that although he cometh now to Church and executeth his function as herein is mentioned yet doth hee the sayd Hugh Reeve manifest himselfe in hart to be a papist by his ordinary conversacon wih a great number of papists not to convert but rather to confirme them, broaching and mayntaining (even to rage) many and sundry popish opinions both in his ordinary discourse and in the pulpit, and by his usuall gestures when he cometh into the Church, as crossing himselfe cringing and ducking and

kneeling at the rayles before the Alter (as he calleth it).

33.   Item that the sayd Hugh Reeve being not long since asked whether when sermons are made by the convocation they ought not to passe with the approbation of the house of Commons, he answered in disdaynfull and arrogant manner, the house of Commons, what have they to do with Cannons, they are not to meddle at all with them I tell you they are not to meddle with them.

34.   Item that he the sayd Hugh Reeve being Surrogate kept a Court without a Register[13] appointed a woman to be his apparitor, and had no proctor but one Dromond his sonne in lawe an excommunicate person and at that Court the sayd Hugh Reeve gave sentence that one Susan Dearman should aske one Tymothy Bayly forgivenasse and did there also acquit one Mrs Williams of a crime of fornication commited with one Throughgood a minister.

35.   Item that still to this very day being the 9th of December 1640, he the sayd Hugh Reeve reads in the Church of Ampthill aforesaid every day in the weeke the prayer made against the invasion of the Scotts and for his Majestys happy returne which as may be conceived doth playnely discover his palpable indiscreation and inveterate mallace against the statte.

36.   Item that he the sayd Hugh Reeve hath often sayd we have to much preaching amongst us there being an lecture performed weekely (in the parish Church of Ampthill) by divers ministers who were conformable to the doctrine of the Church of England, he the sayd Hugh Reeve for the most part when he had read prayers refused to here these Sermons, and went out of the Church when any one of the sayd ministers went up into the pulpit to preach; and this he did in a very arrogant and presumptuous manner; and the reason thereof was because one Mr Beaumond[14] delivered his sermon that the Virgin Mary had noe power to command her sonne to doe any thing.

37.   Item that hee mayntaineth in his ordinary discourse that a minister

which is a Master of Arts ought to take place of any Gentleman a Batchelor of Divinity of any Esquire a Doctor of Divinity of any Knight, a Bishop of any Barron, an Arch-bpp of any Duke, and if there were a Patriarke, he ought so hee sayth, to take place of the King.

38.   Item that one monsieur du Bon[15] a French gentleman being a protestant, and sometimes governor to the nowe Earle of Devonshire was perverted by the sayd Hugh Reeve; as it is vehemently suspected by the sayd Mr du Bon having changed his religion and being in France writt a letter to the sayd Hugh Reeve wherein hee gave him thanks for that he perswaded him to become a Romane Catholicke or words to that effect which letter the sayd Hugh Reeve in a kind of boasting manner showed unto one Mr Barrit a French Gentleman of his acquaintance.

39.   Item that the sayd Hugh Reeve saith hee will mayntaine whatsoever hee hath preached and believes in the same and hath allwayes beene and still is very troublesome amongst his neighbours with suits in the Eclesiasticall courts without any Just cause, and to that purpose he hath preached in the pulpit of the Church of Ampthill aforesayd that hee will spend all that he hath to a groate to defend himselfe and offend others, and that he is carried borne out and boulstered up by a strong faction of Papistes as well within the sayd parish of Ampthill as in divers other places and threatneth all persons within the sayd parish whch dislike his doctrine with suits of law, and hath sued divers of them in the Courts aforesayd, hee being there a surrogate and having a very great party amongst them to bring Grists to their mills.

40.   Item that whereas the sayd Hugh Reeve pretends to be a master of Arts, and by collour thereof (when he read prayers) weares a hood correspondent to that degree, if ever the sayd Hugh Reeve did take that degree hee did never do any exercise for it, but took it at a time when King James of famous memory was at Cambridg, and liberty was given to do it without doing the exercise belonging unto the same Videlicet by a fiat omnes &c as the Schollers use to call it.

41.   Item that the sayd Hugh Reeve hath at sundry times broached and

delivered divers other popish and ridiculous tenetts as in his Lent sermon that the due observance of all fasting and Embering dayes[16] as hee calls them according to the kings laws is a service that God requires at our hands in payne of damnation contrary to the proviso of 5 Eli: 5 and in his sermons upon Easter day that Easter day is the highest Sunday in the yeare; because sayth he the Sunday next following is called Low Sunday, And that at another tyme upon a Christmas day the weather being somewhat cold, he tould his parishioners that he had entended to have given them a sermon but the weather was very cold, and he would have them know that he had a care as well of their bodies as their soules therefore would deferre it till another occasion, and divers other such like stuffe, all which here to relate at large would seeme both tedious & Impertinent [last word deleted 'troublesome' inserted in another hand.]

Parson Reeve, found guilty of being recusant but dealt with "leniently", was deprived of the living, ordered to recant, and awarded a small annuity out of the stipend. A draft warrant drawn up for his arrest does not seem to have been executed and matters muddled on until 1642 when Edmund Wingate approached the House of Lords with a further petition supported by an affidavit restating the original complaints:

The petition of Edmund Wingate

To the Right Honble: the Lords in the
Upper House of Parliament assembled.
The humble Petition of Edmund Wingate Gent:
In behalfe of the Inhabitants of Ampthill
in the County of Bedd:

In all humble manner Sheweth that whereas upon a complaint exhibited by Ben: Rhodes Gent: against Hugh Reeve Clerke, late Parson of Ampthill, for preaching & maintaining divers Popish & unsound opinions, your Lordships by order of the 23 Feb: 1640, did most justly deprive him of all his Ecclesiasticall Livings: And did also order that the house wherein hee the said Reeve dwelt should not be sep[ar]ated from the church of Ampthill, in regard there was no Parsonage house there, nor (indeed) any other house in the towne so fitt for the Incumbent to live in, being a towne house, scituate neare the Church, & wherein the said Reeve hath no estate but at sufferance.

And whereas your Lordships did also farther ordaine that the said Reeve should make a Publique recantation of his grosse errours & that upon the due performance thereof hee should have had paid unto him an Annuitie of ten pounds p.ann during his life, which should have issued out of the Parsonage aforesaid had not a Noble person of the parish[17] freely offered to discharge it himselfe, in regard the said Parsonage is not worth above 30tie pound, as the said Hugh Reeve himselfe hath often reported.

And for as much as the said Hugh Reeve, in manifest contempt of your Lordships said orders doth still continue the possession of the said house, although he hath beene divers times in a faire way required to yeeld up the same, so that the present Incumbent is constrained to hire an other house at a deare rate, and much lesse convenient for his habitation: And lastly in regard the said Hugh Reeve in making his recantation, did rather seeme to maintain than recant his erronious tenets, having also since that time affirmed that he would still maintaine two of those tenets which he then recanted, & that he is still Parson of Ampthill, notwithstanding your Lordships said Order; & (indeede) still manifestly expressing that he is as popishly affected as ever by his daily conversing more than ever with papists, his going out of the church in a contemptuous manner when the rest of the Parish stayde to take the Protestation,[18] his not receaving the Communion for above a Twelve moneth, with divers other apparent signes of his affection to Popery, all which will more clearely appeare by an affidavit hereunto annexed.

Your petitioners humble suite is that your Lordships would be graciously pleased to ordaine that the said Annuity dureing the said Hugh Reeve's life, may be transfered upon the said present Incumbent being a reverent deserving man without exception, & to whome the said Noble Person will be (doubtlesse) more willing to pay it (if it may stand with the good pleasure of this house) than to the said Hugh Reeve, according to the tenor of a Petition heretofore presented to his Lordship by the Inhabitants of Ampthill aforesaid to that purpose: It being most unreasonable (as your petitioner & the said Inhabitants doe humbly conceive) that he the said Reeve should be suffered to take advantage or benefitt of those orders, which he himself hath contemptuously and stubbornely disobayed.   And your Petitoners shall daily pray &c.

Affidavit against Hugh Reeve

Edmund Wingate of Ampthill in the County of Bedd: gentleman maketh oath that Hugh Reeve Clerke late Parson of Ampthill aforesaid,having bene three severall times since the three and twentieth of February 1640 (in a faire way) required by divers of the Inhabitants there, to yield up unto John How Clerke (the present Incumbent) the messuage wherein the said Hugh Reeve then did and still doth dwell, according to an order made by the right Honble. the Lords of the upper house of Parliament (bearing the date the said three and twentieth day of February 1640) hath from time to time forborne to do it, In such sort that the saide present Incumbent (a reverend deserving man) is forced out of that Living (which as the saide Reeve hath often reported to this deponent is not worth above £30 per annum) to give seaven pounds per annum or thereabouts for another house to live in, which (in this deponents opinion) is not neare so convenient for him to dwell in, and at a farther distance from the Church: And farther, that he the said Reeve in making his recantation did rather seeme to maintaine than recant his erronious tenets, And did since his recantation affirm to this deponent that he would still maintain two of those tenets which he then recanted, and that his is still Parson of Ampthill notwithstanding the above said order. And this deponent doth confidently believe, that the said Reeve is still as popishly affected as ever, by his daily conversation with the papists which dwell at Ampthill; by his not receiving the communion at Ampthill since Christmas was twelve months, nor in any other place for any thinge that ever this deponent yet heard, And lastly, by his going out of the Church in a very contemptuous manner upon the fifth of November, when the parishoners there had an order to take the protestation although he the saide Reeve had notice thereof both that day, and also the Sunday before.

Again, all this was ignored by Hugh Reeve, still adamant in the legality of his position as Rector of Ampthill when he made his will on 27 January, 1645/6.

Notes on the Petitions

1   First and Second Table: The division of the Ten Commandments into two sections corresponding to the two tablets of stone brought down from Sinai by Moses concerning duty to God and duty to Man. The Catechism from *The Book of Common Prayer* (1552), which Reeve was obliged to teach his flock, is clear on the latter: "My duty towards my neighbour is ... to submit my selfe to all my governours, teachers, spirituall Pastours and Masters. To order my selfe lowly and reverently to all my betters ..."

2   *Romans* 13 verse 13: "Let us walk honestly, as in the day; not in rioting and drunkenness, not in chambering and wantonness, not in stife and envying." *Philippians* 3 verses 18 & 19: "For many walk, of whom I have told you often, and now tell you even weeping, that they are the enemies of the cross of Christ; Whose end is destruction, whose God is their belly, and whose glory is in their shame, who mind earthly things."

3   Thomas Blyeth. Probably the same of Bedford Street, Ampthill, weaver, buried in 1656.

4   *Psalm* 149 verse 8: "To bind their [the ungodly heathen] kings in chains: and their nobles with links of iron..."

5   The Noble Earle: Thomas Bruce, Earl of Elgin (Chapter 7).

6   Toby Matthew (1546-1628) was Bishop of Durham from 1595 until 1606 when he was translated to York.

7   See published version *Beds Parish Registers Series Vol 17* (Ampthill) page A113

8   Richard Conquest (1597-1671) See Chapter 7.

9   Thomas Cookson, D.D. (Cambridge)   See Chapter 8.

10   John Drommond. See Chapter 8.

11   Mr Watson: Richard Watson (see BHRS Vol 65 page 143). The

Watson family lived at Little Park in Ampthill. Thomas Burges has not been identified.

12   Revill ("Reveile") Reeve was buried at Ampthill, 11 May, 1656.

13   "Without a Register": Does this mean the book, the official or both? In either case the court records of the period are missing. For Drommond see Chapter 8 above. Susan Dearman married Richard Gray at Ampthill in 1640. Why did she have to ask forgiveness of Timothy Bayly? It would be interesting to know more about this case and the other one!

14   Mr Beaumond, perhaps Beaumont? Not traced.

15   "M. du Bon, governor to the nowe Earle of Devonshire..." Lord Elgin's sister, the widowed Countess of Devonshire, lived at Ampthill at this time. See Chapter 7. Mr Barrit, the "French Gentleman" may have been in Lord Elgin's household.

16   "Embering Dayes": Ember Days are the Wednesday, Friday and Saturday after St Lucy (13 December), Ash Wednesday, Whitsunday, and Holy Cross Day (14 September) which are observed in the church as days of fasting and abstinence.

17   "A Noble person of the parish" - Lord Elgin.

18   "The Protestation". In 1641 the House of Commons ordered all males of 18 years and above to subscribe to an oath to oppose the "designs of priests and Jesuits ... to subvert the fundamental laws of the kingdom". The oath was taken at the Gunpowder Plot service that year, and a list of names made. ("A Form of Prayer and Thanksgiving ... for the happy Deliverance of King James I and the Three Estates of England, from the most traiterous and bloody intended Massacre by Gunpowder..." on 5 November, 1605, was attached to *The Book of Common Prayer* until 1859.)

Appendix B

Hugh Reeve's Will

In the name of God Amen. I Hughe Reeve Clerke and the true and lawfull Parson of Ampthull in the Countie of Bedford being weake in bodie by reason of age but in perfect memorie I thank God for the same Doe make and ordaine this my last Will and Testament in manner and forme following. First I give and bequeathe my Soule to God that gave it me though stained with the wayges of synn It being washt in the pretious blood of Christ Jesus and Covered with his white garment of Holinesse and Righteousnesse I present it soe to my sweete Jesus. And my bodie to the earth from whence it came waiting for the holy Resurrection. I praie God to blesse my Children and give them grace to serve God and to hate that which is evil and to love God which is onlie good. And for my worldlie goodys that God hath blessed me withall I will and bequeath as followeth (Memorandum that I gave to my Sonn William Reeve five pounds the first daie of Januarie last) Item I give unto my sonn William Reeve Threescore poundis of Lawfull money of England. Item I give unto my said sonn William Reeve my best Bedstead my best Fetherbed a greene Rugg my greene Curtaines and Vallanse a pillow and pillowbeare a boulster and twoe blanketts. Item I give unto my daughter Revell Reeve fiftie and five poundes of Lawful money of England. Item I give unto my said daughter Revell Reeve a Fetherbed a white Rugg a blankett and a Coverlett a Brasse Pott a Table and three stooles and all the furniture in the Chamber wherein I now lye. Item I give unto my sonn John Reeve Ten poundes of Lawfull mony of England if he the said John be living at the time of my deathe. Item I give unto my Grandchilde Richard Reeve five and twentie pounde of Lawfull mony of England. Item I give unto Amy the wife of Edmund Ruffhead my daughter five poundis of lawfull mony of England. Item I give unto my said daughter Revell Reeve a Bedstead curtaines and vallance one paire

of holland sheetes and a pillow beare and twoe pieces of pewter. Item
I give to my daughter in law William Reeves wife my stuffe Gowne and
my short Cloth Gowne I give unto my daughter Revell Reeve. Item I
give unto John Saunders and Robert Saunders my Gran Children my
long cloth Gowne to make them clothes. Item I give unto my said sonn
William Reeve my deske   Item I give unto my said daughter Amy
Reeve a Canopie. Item I give unto Master Edward Smith twoe and
twentie shillings whom I make overseer of this my last will and Testament.
All the rest of my goods debts and creditts unbequeathed (my debts
being paid and Funerall expenses dischardged and legacies performed)
my Will is the same shal be equallie divided between my said sonn William
Reeve my said daughters Amy and Revell and my said Grandchild Richard
Reeve. And I make my son in lawe Edmund Ruffhead executor of this
my last will and testament Revoking and Annulling all other Wills Legacies
and bequests by me formerly made. Item I give unto Lydia the wife of
the said Edward Smith five shillings to buy her a paire of Gloves. And I
give unto my Godson John Smith six Shillings and eight pence to buy him
an Ewe lambe   In witness whereof I the said Hugh Reeve have hereunto
sett my hand and seale the seaven and twentieth daie of Januarie in the
one and twentieth yeare of the Raiyne of our Soveruiyne Lord King
Charles of England Scotland Fraunce and Ireland Anno Domini one
Thousand Six hundred Forty and five.

Hugh Reeve. Read puplished and declared as the last Will and Testament
of the said Hugh Reeve in the presence of ^ Richard Wheeler, William
Underwood.
^ Memorandum that the saide interlinings were made before the
publyshinge hereof.

Probate was granted to his son-in-law Edmund Ruffhead on 21st
November 1646. Beds Record Office reference Fac: Prob 11/198/30
Money bequeathed: William £5 + £60, Revell £55, John £10, Ann £5,
Grandson Richard £25, Overseer of will, Edw Smith £1.2s, Lydia Smith
for gloves 5s.0d, Godson Jn Smith for 'Ewe lambe' 6s 8d.
Total: £161.13s8d.

Appendix C

Some Aspects of Daily Life

1. CLERGY DRESS AND BEHAVIOUR

Decency in Apparel enjoined to Ministers: The true, ancient, and
flourishing Churches of Christ, being ever desirous that their Prelacy
and Clergy might be had as well in outward reverence, as otherwise
regarded for the worthiness of their ministry, did think it fit, by a prescript
form of decent and comely apparel, to have them known to the people,
and thereby to receive the honour and estimation due to the special
Messengers and Ministers of Almighty God: we, therefore, following
their grave judgement, and the ancient custom of the Church of England,
and hoping that in time newfangleness of apparel in some factious persons
will die of itself, do constitute and appoint . . . That all . . . Ecclesiastical
Persons . . . shall usually wear in their journeys Cloaks with sleeves,
commonly called Priests' Cloaks, without guards, welts, long buttons, or
cuts.   And no Ecclesiastical Person shall wear any Coif or wrought
Night-cap, but only plain Night-caps of black silk, satin, or velvet.   In all
which particulars . . . our meaning is not to attribute any holiness or
special worthiness to the said garments, but for decency, gravity, and
order, as is before specified.   In private houses, and in their studies, the
said Persons Ecclesiastical may use any comely and scholar-like apparel,
provided that it be not cut or pinkt; and that in public they go not in their
Doublet and Hose, without Coats or Cassocks; and that they wear not
any light-coloured Stockings.   Likewise poor beneficed men and Curates
(not being able to provide themselves long Gowns) may go in short Gowns
of the fashion aforesaid..

Sober Conversation required in Ministers:. No Ecclesiastical Person
shall at any time, other than for their honest necessities, resort to any
taverns or alehouses, neither shall they board or lodge in any such places.
Furthermore, they shall not give themselves to any base or servile labour,
or to drinking or riot, spending their time idly by day or night, playing at

dice, cards, or tables, or any other unlawful games: but at all times convenient they shall hear or read somewhat of the holy Scriptures, or shall occupy themselves with some other honest study or exercise, always doing the things which shall appertain to honesty, and endeavouring to profit the Church of God; having always in mind, that they ought to excel all others in purity of life, and should be examples to the people to live well and christianly, under pain of Ecclesiastical censures, to be inflicted with severity, according to the qualities of their offences.
From Canons 74 and 75 of 1603

2. THE CALENDAR

The Julian calendar, introduced by Julius Caesar in 46BC, was in use at the time of the birth of Christ and continued to be used in England until 1752. In the 6th century the Church devised a system for reckoning the years *Anno Domini,* the year of our Lord, counting backwards to what was believed to be the date of Christ's birth. Unfortunately they miscalculated, stopping several years short of the correct date, which is likely to have been in what we think of as between 7 and 11BC. There was no year 0, the era 'Before Christ' ending with the 1st Year of our Lord, making the beginning of the 21st century 1st January 2001. Historically, the 3rd Christian Millennium will have begun sometime in the 1990s.

At the time of the fixing *Anno Domini* New Year's Day was moved to 25th March, Lady Day, the feast of the Annunciation when Mary was told she was to be the mother of Christ. This enabled Christmas Day to fall nine months after the annunciation, although Christ is more likely to have been born sometime in September!

By 1582 the Julian Calendar was ten days behind the astronomical calendar (it is now 13 days behind and is still used by the Orthodox churches) so Pope Gregory XIII introduced a new calendar which jumped 10 days to catch up with science. This Gregorian calendar, which took New Year's day back to 1st January, was not adopted in England until nearly 200 years later, in 1752 (but not in Scotland and

Ireland, although the Scots adopted 1ˢᵗ January as New Year's Day). Some historians prefer to 'modernise' January to March dates from before 1752, others stick to the common use of the period and put years under both calendars – thus, the execution of King Charles I took place on 30ᵗʰ January 1648/9.

3. FOOD AND DRINK – SOME TRADITIONAL RECIPES
The following might (or might not) be based on 17ᵗʰ century originals, and must be tried at the maker's own risk.

KATTERN CAKES In the old days it was customary for Ampthill people to bake and eat what were called Kattern Cakes in commemoration of the good Queen.   Some sources, while associating the cakes with the Queen say they were prepared for the feast of the saint, but whether that was Catherine of Alexandria (Catherine Wheels – 25ᵗʰ November), Catherine of Bologna (9ᵗʰ March) or Catherine of Siena (30ᵗʰ April) is not clear.   Others suggest it was 17ᵗʰ August, the day in 1533 when Queen Katherine left Ampthill for the last time.

Take 2 lb bread dough, knead in 2oz butter or home-made lard, 1oz caraway seed, 2oz sugar and one egg (some recipes omit the egg). When thoroughly mixed allow to stand for ½ hour in a warm place and covered with a cloth.   Bake in a floured baking tin in a moderate oven.

TANDER'S CAKES honouring S.Andrew (30ᵗʰ November), were made along similar lines except that 1 lb dough was mixed with ¼ lb lard, ¼ lb sugar, ¼ lb currants, lemon peel and one egg. (No caraway seeds!) Again, some recipes omit the egg.

From a note by AGU in the pew leaflet 8ᵗʰ Jan 1984, prior to the unveiling of Queen Katherine's window in Ampthill Church, 19ᵗʰ February, 1984.

BEDFORDSHIRE CLANGER (Small size). Take 2½ lb plain flour, 10 oz. suet (water to mix it with). 1 ½ lb streaky pork (diced), ½ lb potatoes (sliced). ½ lb onions (sliced), 2 teaspoonsful parsley (chopped fine), pepper and salt, any sharp tasting jam. (A large saucepan or iron boiler is needed.) Mix flour and suet into crust. Roll the crust out to thickness of half an inch. Spread the meat, etc, evenly over three—quarters width of the crust. Then, very carefully allowing an inch between the two parts, spread jam on the remaining quarter. Roll very carefully and fix a cord between the meat and jam and pull it tight. This keeps the parts separate. Boil water in saucepan. Dip a cloth in the water, ring it out and sprinkle with flour. Wrap the clanger in the cloth [often the wife's wedding stockings – while they lasted] and boil steadily for five hours. Eat hot or cold.

Mrs Dorothy Wooding of The Chequers, Millbrook, in the Ampthill News 27th September 1967

MEAD Take five gallons of water, add to that one gallon of the best honey; set it on the fire, boil it together well and skim it very clean: then take it off the fire, and set it by: then take two or three roots of ginger, the like quantity of cinnamon and nutmegs, bruise all these grossly, and put them in a little Holland bag in the hot liquor, and let it stand until it be cold: then put as much ale-yeast to it as will make it work. Keep it in a warm place as they do ale; and when it hath wrought well, tun it up [put in a cask]; at two months you may drink, having been bottled a month. If kept four months it is better still. *From a cookery book of the year 1803 quoted by Ampthill historian Miss M.S.F.George in the Ampthill News, 29th April,1958.*

4. MONEY
In this period pounds, shillings and pence were in general use. Thomas Arnold (page 48) still used the mark (at its highest two thirds of a pound - 13s 4d:). Urien Maynard, yeoman, left his three godchildren 'Ten groats apees Being Lawfully demanded' in 1642, the groat being worth four pence. (For colloquial use in Parson Reeve's sermon, see page 89.) No attempt has been made to convert money to a modern equivalent – an unrealistic exercise.

Editing & Sources

Spelling: 390 family names (excluding strangers and royalty) were extracted from Hugh Reeve's parish register for this study. Many came in a wide variety of spellings but have been standardised in the most frequently used or less flamboyant variant. Elsewhere, in quotations spelling has not been modernised (except in most place names) as it is felt the writers speak more clearly through their phonetic attempts. However, some contractions have been expanded and the 'y' has been written 'th' where appropriate.

Abbreviations: In the reference section standard publications and works of reference are named in full on the first use, with subsequent abbreviated form in square brackets. The reference to AGU's collection is given where the source is not available in the Bedfordshire County Record Office [BRO].

Wills: References to wills are not given as they are easily found in the BRO card index.

Major sources for this study are two surveys of the manor, one of 1542 the other 1649, and two maps one mid to late 16th century the other by John Davis, 1743 (BRO Fac X1/77, Fac 1 E317, CRT 100/16,24, R1/1). There were no significant changes in the town's layout or setting between Tudor times and the early 19th century.

The Bruce manuscripts are now in the Wiltshire and Swindon Record Office at Trowbridge, but material copied in Bedford (including the magnificent Houghton House household account books and Lord Ailesbury's memoir manuscript) is in BRO ref Mic 120 & Pt 121. See also CRT 100/36, 190/157. AGU's extensive notes are referred to by file ref (25/) and page number.

The petitions of Benjamin Rhodes and Edmund Wingate are in the care of the House of Lords Record Office (House of Lords Main Papers 16 Jan 1640/41 and 30 April 1642 respectively) and are reproduced here with the permission of the Clerk of the Records. They were published (with comment by the present writer) in *Beds Historical Record Society* Volume 72, 1993.

References & Notes

[1] The broket, or brook, was Duck Riddy, then quite an obstacle with ramshackle bridge, but now piped under the road by Gas House Lane.

[2] *Bedfordshire Through Visitors' Eyes* by Simon Houfe (Book Castle) for Hentzer diary. Warren etc: *Bedfordshire Historical Record Society* publications [BHRS] 39 p xxxii. 1611 agreement Beds Record Office [BRO] R.Box 1: prison sentence BRO QSR 1726-104. The Warren Account for 1746 (BRO RO) though outside the period of this study gives some indication of its size and success. '. . . Rabbits killed & sold . . . at 7s per dozen from 14th Dec 1745 to 23rd Jan 1745 . . . in all twenty seven Dozen and nine Rabbits which . . . is £9:14:3d The Warren tackle as netts Steel traps . . a pair of Baskets for Carring out Rabbits . . . A ferret hutch . . . seven steel traps.' John Rissley the warrener was paid 10s a week, with extra 4s for 4 night's hunting. His assistant Richard Upton had 7s a week. In 1746 Thomas Cook was paid for two day's work drawing timber from the park to build 'the Watch House on the Warren' thought to be the Wooden House in Oliver St. Members of the Upton family continued to live in what is now 'The Little Cottage' in Meadow Way – then in splendid isolation on the Warren – until well into the 19th century.

[3] BRO H.S.A. 1668ff AGU 6/2, 6/3, 6/5

[4] Lammas, 1st August – Loaf Mass – the pre-reformation harvest festival when the bread used in the mass was made from flour ground from the first corn of the season. This was probably the field where the earliest harvesting could be expected.

[5] Public Record Office [PRO] E134 Bundle 25. Gladys Scott Thomson writing in *'Ampthill: Honour, Manor, Park . . .'* (British Archaeological Assoc *Journal* 1950) credits the discovery of the map in the PRO to Miss Lilian Redstone, but gives it an earlier date in the 1540s or 1550s.

[6] On the site of what is now 1, 3 & 5 Church Street. In the 1850s the rose rent was due annually to the Lord of the Manor, presumably, but a century later, when the present writer's parents owned the property, the requirement had long been forgotten. For Bury Piece rent – 1682 – see AGU25/44. For Barnacles, 1671 AGU3/3.

[7] Appears in 1467-8 rental when the manor was held by the de Greys. BHRS 46 p 106.

[8] Nine public spirited Ampthill worthies are known to have left bequests for Hazelwood Lane's repair and upkeep in their wills between 1505 and 1549 and there were doubtless similar gestures through the period.

122

⁹ 18th century Ampthillians would be totally bemused at their present day successors' efforts to expose hidden timbers and open up great fireplaces. 'Blind' windows in Georgian facades usually indicate earlier interiors not matching up with symmetrical new frontages and hardly ever an avoidance of window tax. It would have cost more to brick up the window than pay the tax.
¹⁰ AGU 36/41.

¹¹ Simon Urlin's wife Ann died in 1681, aged 26, and the sad memorial to her and three of her five daughters is in the church. Simon Urlin moved across the road to Humphrey Iremonger's old house in Church Square (now Dynevor House) which he remodelled - his initials SV and the date 1725 can be seen on the rainwater heads.
¹² AGU 3/3, 25/46 & 54.
¹³ PRO calendar *Letters & Papers of Henry VIII* Vol 5 p1187.
¹⁴ *Select Illustrations of Bedfordshire*, the Revd J.D.Parry, 1827, page 72 The site of the gateway can be picked out in the ground just east of trees north of the fence behind cricket pitch. (The castle cries out for professional archaeological excavation at the earliest opportunity!)
¹⁵ PRO E 314/25 quoted in the British Archaeological Assoc *Journal p 17*. (see note 6 above).
¹⁶ BHRS 71. In 1536 Henry's army had been summoned to Ampthill in readiness for a confrontation with the Pilgrimage of Grace rebels. 40,000 soldiers were expected and 19,394 had arrived when the rebels negotiated, so to save expense troops en route were sent straight back home. The chaos in Ampthill and around at the time is hard to imagine. See *The Lisle Letters,* Muriel St.Clare Byrne, (University of Chicago Press) 1981 Vol 3 p252.
¹⁷ BHRS 18 p 12. For details of the Duke of Bedford's camp see *Around Ampthill* page 34.
¹⁸ PRO *Calendar Patent Rolls* 1553 p 209, 211 (AGU 33/18). BHRS 5 p 77. *Beds Notes & Queries* [BNQ] 1/95.
¹⁹ BHRS 16 p118, BHRS 65, pp 143-4, AGU25/4,55.
²⁰ *Victoria County History of Bedfordshire* [VCH] 3/288ff.
²¹ The best history of Houghton House's occupants is the series by M.S.F.George in *Beds Magazine* Volume 1. See also BHRS 74 where James Collett-White gives the most balanced analysis of the arguments surrounding its architectural history. (John Aubrey in his *Brief Lives* – ed Oliver Lawson Dick, 1949, Secker & Warburg - said it had been built by Italians.) See also AGU's *Ampthill a Goodly Heritage* (1976) particularly chapters 7 and 8. At one time there was a fresco representing 'a game-keeper, or woodman, taking aim with a cross-bow, full front, with some curious perspective scenery, 6 feet by 9½ feet' – Parry *op*

cit p71 - said to have been James I in disguise. When the house was dismantled the painting was transferred to canvas by Robert Salmon and hung in Park House but has since been lost.

[22] Mrs Margaret McGregor's invaluable introduction to the BRO's RO catalogue.

[23] VCH 3/271

[24] D. & S. Lysons' *Magna Britannia* Vol 1 (1806) p36 gives PRO refs for the market charters of 1219 (Fin Rot 3 Hen III) and 1242 (C 26 Hen III). An early MSS copy of the latter is in BRO R Box 3.

[25] Formerly residing in what became 31-35A Church Street. Ambrose Samm had been John Okey's bailiff. 18th century Samms lived in what after 1860 became 25 & 27 Church Street, but has now been restored into one house.

[26] Another small boy in the crowd in the 1650s might have been Thomas Underwood who became a market gardener at Water End in Maulden, and left the Church of England. He was the present writer's 6x great grandfather and is thought to have been the son of William Underwood who lived in Ampthill and married Ann King in 1640 – and was one of the witnesses to Hugh Reeve's will in 1645.

[27] BHRS 20.

[28] *Beds Mag* Vol 7 p 304/5 1960-61. Also BNQ 1 p 4.

[29] BHRS 31 p 80.

[30] AGU45/4(1)

[31] The Rezzy in the park was created in the 1770s.

[32] BRO BS 818.

[33] AGU 25/2,6,7,19 1670s. *Book of Days*, ed R.Chambers, 1863. Entry 24th June. For the story of John the Baptist, Luke 1

[34] *Bedfordshire Parish Registers* [BPRS] Vol 17 ed F.G.Emmison (1938) page A113. For Steppingley incident see BPRS 50 p 56.

[35] It was customary to celebrate by hanging garlands of branches cut from trees and the hedgerows outside the fronts of houses, much as pennants and flags are flown today.

[36] Tipcat 'a game in which a player strikes a tapered piece of wood at one end, causing it to spring up, before hitting it away'. *Oxford English Dictionary* New Shorter edn. 1993

[37] Undated press cutting AGU 20D45. AGU 25/7, 25/41, 25/44

[38] Bruce MSS 862 p 30 (AGU 25/91) undated but c1680 account refers to the fire without giving a date. In 1679 Hampton in Arden responded to an appeal by brief (*Ampthill Parish Mag* June 1950). I am grateful to Chris Pickford, formerly Beds County Archivist now Director, Church of England Record Centre, for this information and drawing my attention to the 'rare and weighty tome' *Church*

Briefs by W.A.Bewes (1896).

[39] AGU 25/118.

[40] Account from parliamentarian news-sheet *Mercuricus Britannicus* which tells of Capt Temple receiving a jacket from one of the troop who knew him, and his escape after unhorsing his guard and swimming a river. See AGU's *Ampthill Bedside Book I* p27.

[41] BRO BS 224, BHRS 18.

[42] *History of Milton Keynes & District Vol I,* Sir Frank Markham, 1973. (White Crescent Press).

[43] The Great Lodge incident, reported in Halstead's *Succinct Genealogies* 1685, p 410, was discovered by Simon Houfe and appears in his *Bedfordshire Through Visitors' Eyes*. Op cit. I am most grateful to Mr Houfe for his help in trying to identify Edward Harris (note 49 below) and in investigating the engravers of the Houghton House illustrations, p.28 & Pl 1.

[44] In 1955 a Charles I farthing was found amongst the fragments of medieval glass from these windows excavated from the churchyard. (AGU 45/4(1).)

[45] BPRS 17 pA113: AGU 25/47.

[46] Original register BRO ref P30/1/1.

[47] See *The Parish Chest* W.E.Tate (CUP) p 46

[48] BRO CRT 170/9/7 for 1676 survey - 339 Church of England, one papist and [24] non-conformists. An estimate of 599 inhabitants, based on the Hearth Tax returns of 1671 (BHRS 16) is probably a bit high. (The first national census was not until 1801 when the town had 1,234 inhabitants.)

[49] For Chris Grey see *Ampthill Church Bells* by Chris Pickford, 1980. Edward Harris the limner has not been traced (see note 43 above).

[50] BRO L26/9.

[51] BRO ABC5 (translated by Patricia Bell) AGU45/4(20). BNQ 3 pp 36-40.

[52] William Nash was buried on 4th June, 1607, and on 4th October in the same year, Agnes Noone married George Warlowe – with her mother's approval, it is hoped, although the fact of the proviso in the will suggests trouble had been looming. Francis Lord Russell was given custody of lands in Ampthill and elsewhere on behalf of Edmund son of Edmund Conquest, deceased, during his minority. This was four years after the grant of Woburn Abbey to Russell, so one of the Russell family's earliest connections with Ampthill. PRO *Calendar Patent Rolls 1551* p110 (iv) – AGU 33/18.

[53] BHRS 74 p103. *Dictionary of National Biography* [DNB]. John Aubrey's *Brief Lives* op cit, AGU's *Goodly Heritage* op cit p 28.

[54] *Beds Mag* 1p 83 1947/8 M.S.F.George article based on *The Table Book*, ed W.Hone (1864) p 527ff.

[55] *The Life & Loyalties of Thomas Bruce* by the Earl of Cardigan, 1951 (Routledge & Kegan Paul).

[56] *The Life of the Right Honourable and Religious Lady Christian Late Countess Dowager of Devonshire.* London. Printed by William Rawlins for the Author (Thomas Pomfret) 1685. British Library 1112c3. Spelling retained, but some commas and a great many capital letters removed.

[57] DNB (J.A.Doyle.) The work in New York by Ampthill's most distinguished son is outside the scope of this study. A full biography is long overdue. The three Nicolls brothers remained unmarried, but generations of proud Americans have claimed descent from Governor Nicolls's brother Francis, unscrupulous 19th century genealogists having equated a Sergeant Francis born in 1595, with the Governor's brother Francis, born in 1620.

[58] See particularly Margaret McGregor's introduction to file RO5 in BRO, and her 'The Conquest Family of Houghton Conquest', *Beds Mag* 14 p167 1974. Also, 'Beds Armorial – Conquest' by F.W.Kuhlicke, *Beds Mag* 7 p 120 1960.

[59] BHRS 49 p 88. See also BHRS 65 where the author queries the absence of household goods from an inventory of Richard Conquest's possessions. Could it be that they had all been sold for ready cash? The wealth of most country families was tied up in land with rents usually outstanding.

[60] *Canon 66* of 1603. Articles 22 & 23 of the petition to parliament also refer to his being a magistrate, no longer possible for a Roman Catholic.

[61] AGU 25/115.

[62] Peter Samwaies (1615-1693) MA, DD. Royalist divine. Prebendary of York 1668. [DNB] His *Narration* in Rhodes's memory ignores the instructions of the *Directory* (Page 57).

[63] The parish registers of Ampthill, Maulden, Houghton Conquest and Clophill show an abnormally high death rate in 1657 - 31, 30, 28, and 18 respectively, the average rate for the previous/following three years being 19/14, 18/20, 11/21 and 11/18. The total deaths in the 4 parishes for 1657 are 16 (Nov), 14 (Aug, Sept, Dec), 11 (May, Oct), 8 (Apr, Jan), 3 (Mar), 2 (Jul, Feb), 1 (Jun). What happened in 1657 to cause the high death rate is a mystery, but in September of that year Robert Bruce (away from home) received a letter from his cousin Lord Devonshire 'I find a desire both of my Uncle and Mother, that you should continue with me 3 weekes longer, because there has beene so much sicknesse at Ampthill, that soone the howse will not be fit to receave you . . . 'AGU 25/131.

[64] DNB 1921-22 reprint. Okey letter BRO FN 1227. S.Andrew's having survived the Great Fire, was rebuilt (by Wren) in 1686, but burnt out in the blitz, 1941

[65] BHRS 35, 1955 by Gordon Tibbutt (1912-1982). [Author's note: Gordon Tibbutt was a family friend whom I got to know when he was researching this volume.

126

He encouraged my interest by sending copies of all his articles, and the first 3 pictures in my collection were of John Okey, received in 1943 – when I was nine – and still in the collection, 34D, 34E, & 34F.]

66 The Mormon International Genealogical Index [IGI] lists three Hugh Reeves born in 1560, which is too early for our man. A more likely candidate is the Hugh son of John Reeve christened at Cowlinge, Suffolk, on 24th October, 1566. The will of John Reeve of Cowlinge, 1607, (Suffolk RO R2/46/114) does not mention a son Hugh, but does mention testator's deceased brother also John – whose will cannot be traced – who was presumably the father of the 1566 Hugh. Two Johns in one generation is not extraordinary, but the fact that Hugh and Ann also had two Johns is perhaps more than coincidence. It is possible that our Hugh is none of these – we shall never know. (I am grateful to Dr Peter Wothers of St Catharine's College, Cambridge, for searching - though unfruitfully - the surviving records of Mandate degree awards in the University Library.)

67 BNQ 3 p 318. Lincoln Archive Office PD 1600/11, Presentation PD 1600/36.

68 Queen Elizabeth's views on married clergy, *The Curate's Lot* A.Tindal Hart 1970 (John Baker) p 64.

69 BNQ 1p144, Articles to parliament 34 & 39. 1708 terrier AGU 45/1.

70 2nd Act of Uniformity 1562.

71 BRO CRT 130.

Index People & Places

(Illustrations in bold type)

128

Hodgkis Rich, Eliz, Arth 16,17,32,83
HOLLAND 72,73
Holland Rd 13
Hollidaie Thos 23
HOLLINGTON BRIDGE 19, 20
Hollis Alex, Wm 56 Fra 68
Holt Ron 5, **47**
Honour Tom 19
Hop Ground 36
Hospital (Ampthill – Jn Cross) 18, 42
Houfe Simon 121, 124
HOUGHTON CONQUEST 15, 19,
    27, 28, 50, 71, 78-80, 82, 104, 125
    Bury Fm 28 Bury **Pl 8**
HOUGHTON HOUSE 15, 18, 19, **28,**
    27-30, 33-37, 42, 43, 47, 61, 62, 72-
    74, 77, 81, 122, 123, **Pl 1**
HOW GREEN – see EWE GREEN
Howe Jn 57,111
Hudson Wm 14,18
HUNTINGDON 34
ICKWELL 32
Inns – see under individual name
IRELAND 23, 102
Iremonger Humph 45, 122 Wm 45
IRNHAM Lincs 79,80
James Mr of Kent 105
James I 10, 22, 25, 28-30, 33, 41, 44,
    53, 72, 73, 79, 87, 108, 113, 122.
    Jas II 17, 44 (Dk of York 77)
Jeffrey Wid 18
John of Ampthill 19
Jones Jn 41
Jonson Ben 73
Katherine of Aragon, Queen 10, 22,
    37, 97. Kattern Cakes 118
Kellow Eliz 67
Kilby Jn 62
KIMBOLTON Hunts - castle 10
King Ann 123
King's Arms 33 Yard 38, **Pl 6**
King's Head 33
KINGS LYNN Norfolk 62

Kirby Thos 11, 48
Knoll - see Galley Nolle
Kuhlicke Fredk Wm 125
Lambert Wm 23
Lammas 121 Lammas Ground 12
LANCASTER Pr Elizabeth of 21, 48
Lane Jn 63
Laud Wm, Archbp 50, 52, 88, 90
LEIGHTON BUZZARD 52
Leland Jn 9, 10, 22, 23, 25
Lime Rd 13
LINCOLN Bps of 10, 52, 86-88, 90,
    105 Diocese 52, 55, 104
Lines Thos 62
Ling Hills 13 (see The Firs & The
    Moors)
Lodge House (Houghton Pk) 18
Lodington Jn & Margt 49
LONDON 19, 32, 34, 62, 97 Bp of 90
    Downing St 85 Fire of 42, 126
    Grays Inn 83, 84 Holborn 84
    Newgate Market 11 Smithfield 20
    Tower of 20, 52, 76, 84, 85
    Tyburn 85
Long Close 12
Lucas Caesar 69 Hen 69
Luke Sir Oliver 38
Luther Martin 97
LUTON 19, 20, 34, 44, 45, 75
Lyffyn Wm 64
Lysons D & S 24
Market Sq/Pl 15, 56 Cross 15, 39
    House 32
Markham Sir Frank 124
MARSTON MORETEYNE 94
Mary Tudor (Queen) 26, 44, 98
Matthew Toby Bp Durham 86, 112
MAULDEN 11, 13, 14, 19, 38, 62,
    71, 82, 83, 123, 125 Bruce
    Mausoleum 80, 82 **Pl 8** Rd
    Ampthill 18
Maynard Urien 119
Meadow Way 121

Subject Index

By the same author
'Home Rule for Ampthill' (Urban District Council 1974)
Ampthill 'a Goodly Heritage' (Parochial Church Council 1976)
Ampthill in Old Picture Postcards
(European Library, Zaltbommel 1-1988, 2-1989, 3-1994)
Guide and short history *Around Ampthill* 1992, 1997
Ampthill Church from 1955, 6th edition 1996

Also *Bedford Modern School of the Black & Red*
(BMS 1981)
etc.

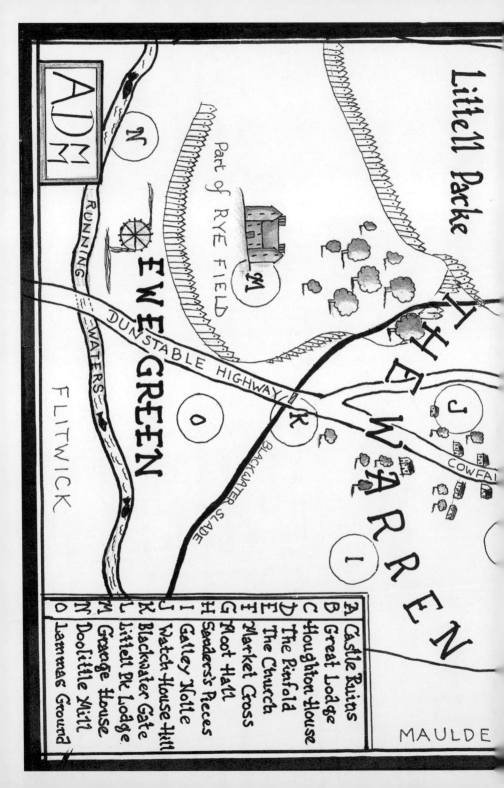